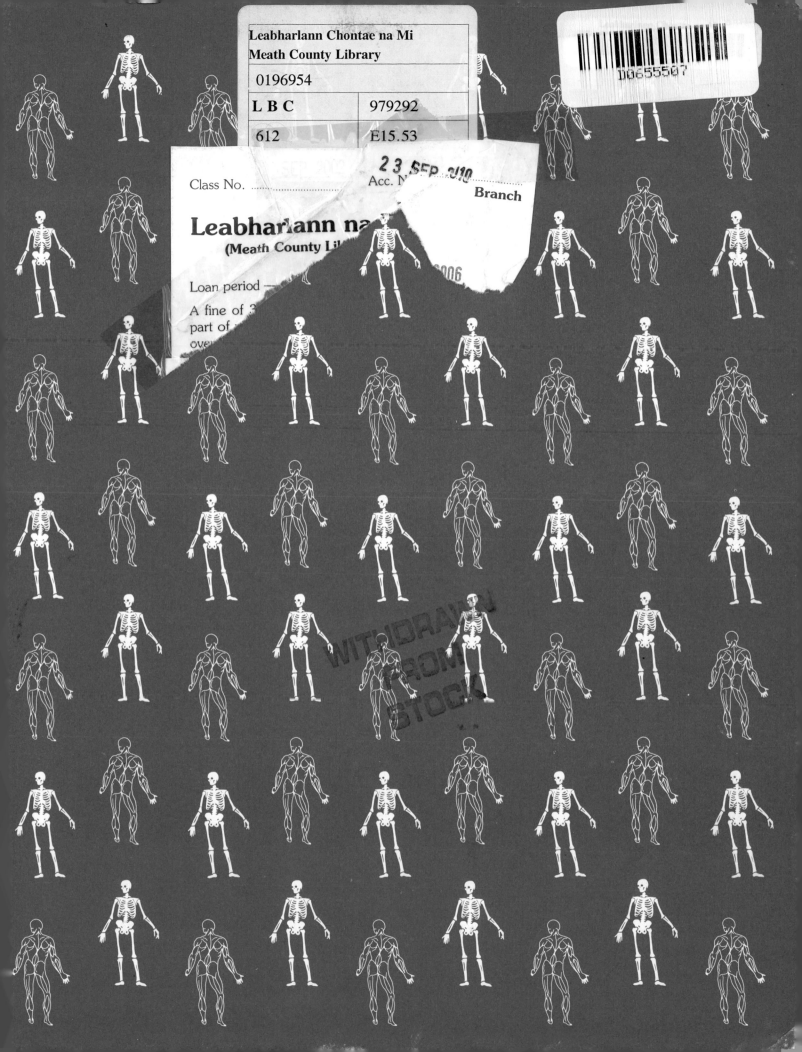

EYEWITNESS ⟨◉⟩ GUIDES

HUMAN BODY

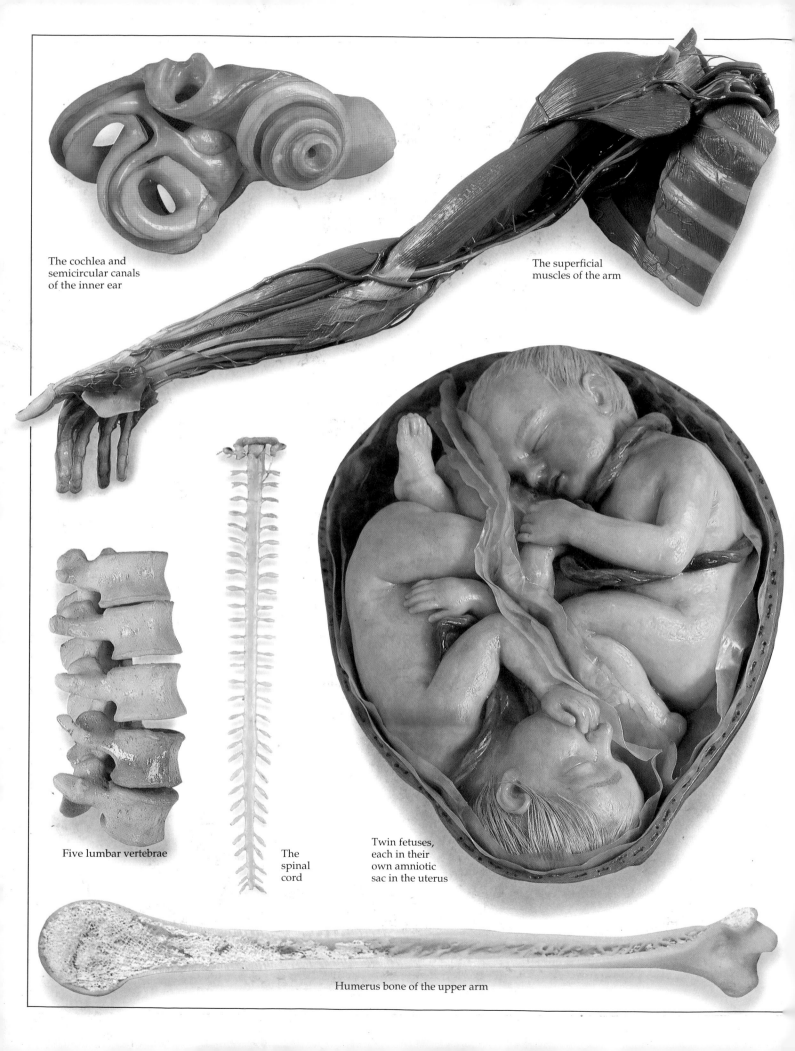

The cochlea and semicircular canals of the inner ear

The superficial muscles of the arm

Five lumbar vertebrae

The spinal cord

Twin fetuses, each in their own amniotic sac in the uterus

Humerus bone of the upper arm

The heart is a
dual pump

EYEWITNESS GUIDES

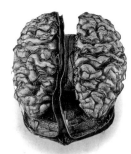

The brain, seen
from above

HUMAN
BODY

Written by
STEVE PARKER

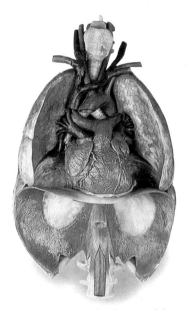

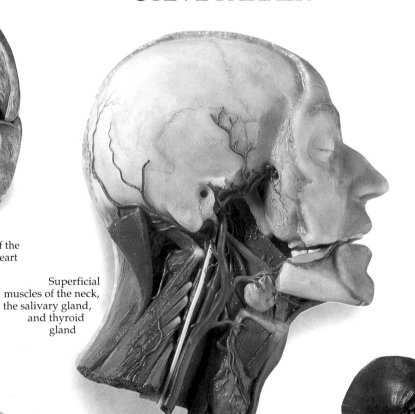

The lungs and diaphragm of the
respiratory tract, with the heart

Superficial
muscles of the neck,
the salivary gland,
and thyroid
gland

Fresh blood, and blood
allowed to settle out

Thick skin covers
the heel of the foot

The liver,
gall bladder,
and stomach

DK

DORLING KINDERSLEY
LONDON • NEW YORK • STUTTGART

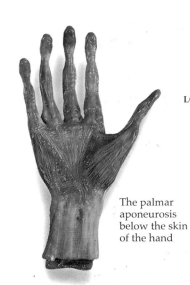

The palmar
aponeurosis
below the skin
of the hand

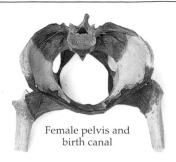

Female pelvis and
birth canal

DK

Dorling Kindersley

LONDON, NEW YORK, AUCKLAND, DELHI, JOHANNESBURG, MUNICH,
PARIS, and SYDNEY

For a full catalogue, visit

 www.dk.com

Ribs and intercostal muscles
involved in breathing

Project editor Liz Wheeler

Art editor Thomas Keenes

Design assistant Helen Diplock

Production Louise Daly

Picture research Diana Morris

Managing editor Josephine Buchanan

Managing art editor Lynne Brown

Special photography Liberto Perugi

Editorial consultant Dr Frances Williams

This Eyewitness ® Guide
first published in Great Britain in 1993 by
Dorling Kindersley Limited, 9 Henrietta Street,
London WC2E 8PS

2 4 6 8 10 9 7 5 3 1

Copyright © 1993
Dorling Kindersley Limited, London

A CIP catalogue record for this book is available
from the British Library

ISBN 0-7513-6142-9

Colour reproduction by Colourscan, Singapore
Printed in China by Toppan Printing Co. (Shenzhen) Ltd.

Blood
circulation in
the leg and foot

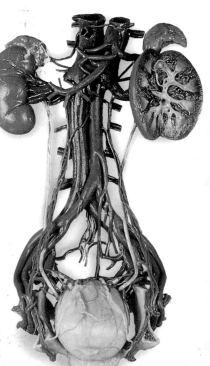

Kidneys, ureters, bladder,
and blood supply of the
male urinary system

Contents

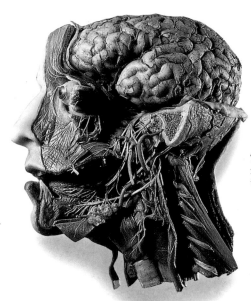

The brain and
nerve supply to
the head and neck

The human body

ARISTOTLE OF ANCIENT GREECE, who had one of the world's greatest minds, taught that only by knowing the origin of something can it be truly understood. Modern biology and evolutionary theory suggest that today's humans began to evolve from creatures similar to chimpanzees, some 5 to 10 million years ago. By 3 million years ago these distant ancestors were walking upright, but were still small and small-brained. Fossils show that through a series of steps the body grew larger, and the brain evolved faster still. The latest genetic studies indicate that all modern humans, species *Homo sapiens*, may well have originated from a group of people in eastern or southern Africa, some 150,000 years ago. From here they spread around the globe, multiplying in numbers, and gradually making more and more extensive changes to their surroundings. Today there are well over 5,000 million human bodies on the planet. Like other mammals, they have warm blood, hair covering their bodies, and produce milk to feed their young.

A SENSE OF BEAUTY
The Kiss, by French sculptor Auguste Rodin (1840-1917), celebrates the beauty of the human form. Rodin shook the world of sculpture with a "back to nature" approach. He represented the body with such astonishing accuracy that he was accused of making plaster casts of real people.

A SENSE OF SURROUNDING
A basic animal characteristic is the ability to sense the surrounding world, in order to find food, shelter, and mates, and to avoid getting into dangerous situations. This 19th-century painting depicts the body's five major ways of doing this: the senses of sight, hearing, smell, taste, and touch. For humans they have long since ceased to aid just basic survival. They are now also employed in the pursuit of knowledge, and to make life more pleasurable.

A SENSE OF UNDERSTANDING
The structure of the human body is known as its anatomy. How the body works is termed physiology. These are two sides of the same coin. Their scientific study dates back chiefly to the Renaissance period, in the 15th and 16th centuries. It was really only after these centuries that the body was cut open, or dissected, and its parts examined in minute detail. These illustrations are from a monumental book by the "founder" of scientific anatomy, Andreas Vesalius (p. 10) from Brussels.

Muscular system (pp. 20-21)

Skeletal system (pp. 14-15)

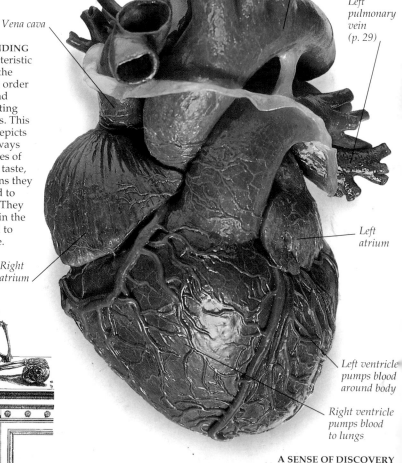

Windpipe is the air passage in breathing

Arch of aorta carries blood to lower body (p. 29)

Left pulmonary vein (p. 29)

Vena cava

Left atrium

Right atrium

Left ventricle pumps blood around body

Right ventricle pumps blood to lungs

A SENSE OF DISCOVERY
Newcomers to anatomy may be surprised to discover that the body's interior is not a thick soup, or continuous meat-like flesh. It is divided into discrete (separate) organs, like this model of a heart (pp. 28-29), that make up a complex three-dimensional maze. Most of the organs can be eased away from their neighbours, except for their vital connections, which include blood vessels and nerves.

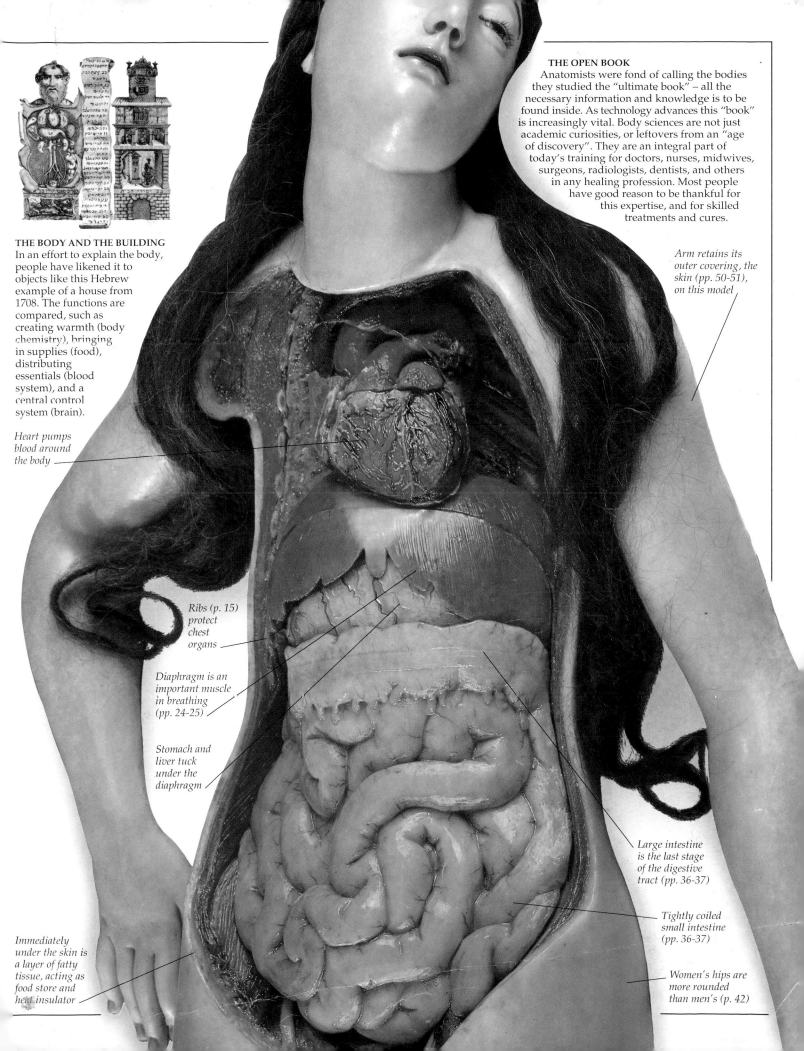

THE BODY AND THE BUILDING
In an effort to explain the body, people have likened it to objects like this Hebrew example of a house from 1708. The functions are compared, such as creating warmth (body chemistry), bringing in supplies (food), distributing essentials (blood system), and a central control system (brain).

Heart pumps blood around the body

Ribs (p. 15) protect chest organs

Diaphragm is an important muscle in breathing (pp. 24-25)

Stomach and liver tuck under the diaphragm

Immediately under the skin is a layer of fatty tissue, acting as food store and heat insulator

THE OPEN BOOK
Anatomists were fond of calling the bodies they studied the "ultimate book" – all the necessary information and knowledge is to be found inside. As technology advances this "book" is increasingly vital. Body sciences are not just academic curiosities, or leftovers from an "age of discovery". They are an integral part of today's training for doctors, nurses, midwives, surgeons, radiologists, dentists, and others in any healing profession. Most people have good reason to be thankful for this expertise, and for skilled treatments and cures.

Arm retains its outer covering, the skin (pp. 50-51), on this model

Large intestine is the last stage of the digestive tract (pp. 36-37)

Tightly coiled small intestine (pp. 36-37)

Women's hips are more rounded than men's (p. 42)

In the image of the gods

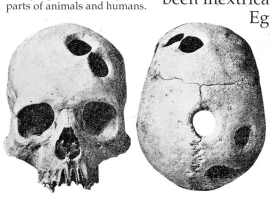

Mᴏʀᴇ ᴛʜᴀɴ 30,000 ʏᴇᴀʀs ᴀɢᴏ the human body was depicted in prehistoric sculptures and in images painted on cave walls around the world. People had an awareness of body shape and form. They lived close to nature, and they saw that their own inner anatomy must resemble that of the beasts they hunted, while butchering them to cook and eat. Gradually civilization brought the opportunity to study anatomy and physiology more methodically. This was not so much a quest for knowledge but a necessity for healing the sick, treating the injured, and preserving the body for the return of its departed soul. Since those early times, medicine has been inextricably bound up with religion, magic, and superstition. The Egyptians made mummies by the million, but little of their purely anatomical knowledge has survived. The Greeks and Romans began to study human structure and function for its own sake, as well as for medical application. Hippocrates (around 460-400 ʙᴄ) and Aristotle (384-322 ʙᴄ) of Greece, and the Roman Galen (ᴀᴅ 129-199), were among the great pioneers.

HOLES IN THE HEAD
Many thousands of years ago in the New Stone Age, people cut holes in the skull with rock knives to expose the brain. This was probably as part of a magical ritual, perhaps to let out "evil spirits". Skulls with part-healed holes show people survived the procedure, called trephining. It persisted through the Middle Ages, and is occasionally still used in surgery.

SURGICAL SACRIFICE
Several ancient cultures sacrificed animals and humans to please their gods and spirits. In the 14th and 15th centuries the Aztecs dominated present-day Mexico. They believed their sun-and-war god Huitzilopochtli would make the sun rise and bring them success in battle, if offered daily blood, limbs, and hearts torn from living sacrifices, including people. From such rituals grew their knowledge of the body's inner organs.

EGYPTIAN PRESERVATION
From about 5,500 years ago, the Ancient Egyptians preserved many millions of human bodies as mummies. They believed that the soul was immortal. It left its body at death, but would revisit at some point in the future. Bodies were mummified – prepared by basic surgery, chemical embalming, and drying – and wrapped for preservation. Then they were entombed to await the soul's return.

Hole in mummy's side where internal organs were removed, to preserve separately

Even the facial features have been well preserved

Wrappings removed from mummy reveal leathery skin (pp. 50-51)

CHINESE CHANNELS

Almost 2,300 years ago, the Chinese *Nei Ching* (Medicine of the Yellow Emperor) described some body parts, but generally the Ancient Chinese placed less importance on detailed knowledge of structure. Their medical systems focused on the flow of unseen "chi" energy along body channels known as meridians (left). This helped to balance qualities known as Yin, cool and "female", and Yang, hot and "male". In acupuncture today, needles are inserted into the meridians to restore correct energy flow and rebalance Yin and Yang.

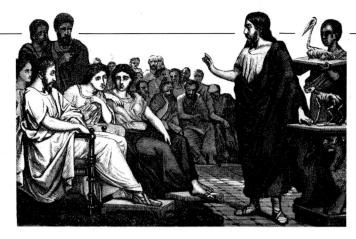

CLADIUS GALEN

Galen of Ancient Rome is a towering figure in the history of anatomy, physiology, and medicine. He was physician to Emperor Marcus Aurelius, and would have seen human innards at first hand as he attended gladiator combats in the arena. Galen made many important discoveries, but he also made great errors. His authority and arrogance, and the succeeding conservative climate of religion and tradition, turned his works into "bibles" of anatomy and medicine for 14 centuries, delaying further progress. He wrote dozens of books, including *On the Use of the Parts of the Human Body*.

Galen, whose often flawed ideas influenced anatomy and medicine for 14 centuries

Hippocrates is often known as the "father of medicine"

MEDIEVAL METHODS

Blood-letting, using a knife or leech, was a traditional and popular, if brutal, remedy for all manner of ills. Few people bothered to see if it actually worked. For centuries there was little organized or thorough assessment of medical treatments, to see if they were of any benefit. Scientific methods, including keeping records and checking up afterwards, were not developed until the last three centuries.

INFLUENCE OF THE ANCIENTS

The influence in Europe of the Roman Catholic Church almost halted scientific progress during the Middle Ages. The teachings of Hippocrates, Aristotle, and Galen survived largely because they were utilized by Arabs from North Africa and the Middle East. One Arab anatomist was Avicenna (AD 980-1037). This title page from a translation of the Sina canon of medicine of 1610 shows the continuing devotion to these great figures.

Leg muscles (pp. 20-21) have wasted away, revealing the shapes of the bones (pp. 14-15)

Avicenna, Persian anatomist, built on the teachings of the Romans and Greeks

Shin and calf bones under skin

Toenails (p. 51) can still be seen after thousands of years

Discussion and dissection

PERHAPS IT IS NOT SURPRISING THAT ARISTOTLE, Galen and other ancient greats made the occasional error. Galen himself cut open and studied the insides of cows, pigs, and apes – but probably not humans. Tradition and religion forbade him. This oppressive attitude deepened during the Middle Ages. Progress in many areas of art, science, and technology was slow, even stagnant. The 15th century saw the dawn of the Renaissance. This "rebirth" and flowering of the arts, architecture, and science spread from Italy across Europe. With fewer religious constraints scientists were able to study with clearer vision. They could record the evidence of their own eyes, rather than blindly repeat the centuries-old established views. Leonardo da Vinci (1452-1519), genius in both art and science, was one of the first to question Galenic tradition. He found that in order to represent the human form in his art, he needed some inside knowledge, and what he saw did not agree with the accepted wisdom of the ancients. Other artists and scientists also began to dissect. This culminated in the revolutionary work of Andreas Vesalius (1514-1564), one of the founders of anatomy.

RESPECT FOR DEATH
For many people in the Middle Ages, life was merely a prelude to what really mattered – death, and ascent into heaven. The body was the soul's temporary home. Earthly matters, like what was inside the body, were unimportant. Dissection was forbidden, and this anatomist may well have been punished.

ANATOMY THEATRE
As the quest for knowledge gained popularity, anatomy theatres were built at numerous universities and centres of learning. Their origins began in law schools, where bodies needed to be cut up for legal reasons in post-mortem examinations. Spectators in the galleries looked down on the professor and the body. An early anatomy professor was Mondinus de Luzzi (1275-1326) at Bologna. Known as the "Restorer of Anatomy", his 1316 book *Anathomia* was the first manual of anatomy and physiology from this new age, even though he still relied heavily on Aristotle and Galen.

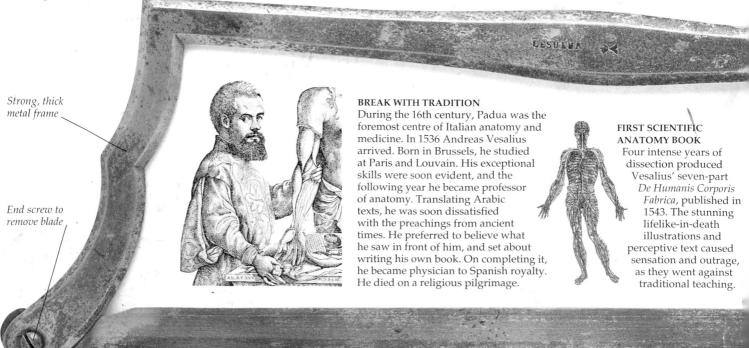

Strong, thick metal frame

End screw to remove blade

BREAK WITH TRADITION
During the 16th century, Padua was the foremost centre of Italian anatomy and medicine. In 1536 Andreas Vesalius arrived. Born in Brussels, he studied at Paris and Louvain. His exceptional skills were soon evident, and the following year he became professor of anatomy. Translating Arabic texts, he was soon dissatisfied with the preachings from ancient times. He preferred to believe what he saw in front of him, and set about writing his own book. On completing it, he became physician to Spanish royalty. He died on a religious pilgrimage.

FIRST SCIENTIFIC ANATOMY BOOK
Four intense years of dissection produced Vesalius' seven-part *De Humanis Corporis Fabrica*, published in 1543. The stunning lifelike-in-death illustrations and perceptive text caused sensation and outrage, as they went against traditional teaching.

SUBJECTS FOR STUDY

Hanged criminals were a steady source of specimens for dissection. In *The Anatomy Lesson of Dr Nicholaas Tulp* (1632), a celebrated painting by Rembrandt (1606-1669) set in Amsterdam, the dissection subject was Aris Kindt. He had stolen clothing – on several occasions! The painting shows a popular view of anatomists, dissecting the flexor muscles of the hand (pp. 22-23). Anatomy lessons were training for physicians and surgeons, and public occasions for anyone interested, from lawyers to merchants and councillors.

WOMEN AND ANATOMY

Until the last century, human structure and function were studied almost exclusively by men. Women figure in exceedingly minor roles, if at all – except for the midwife. This profession has always been almost exclusively female. These Swedish women learning anatomy, in a photograph from about 1880, are probably training for midwifery.

Double-ended small probe

Fine end

Bulbous end

Double-ended medium probe

Cupped end

Finger holes

Hooked point

Hooked needle

Wooden handle

Medium scissors

Blade can be sharpened for use

Rounded tips to blades

Shiny metal finish to aid cleaning

Scalpel

Fine forceps (tweezers)

Long handles improve leverage

Needle-like tips

Ridged, splayed tips for gripping

Clamping forceps

TOOLS OF THE TRADE

Today's surgeons have power-saws, laser-scalpels, micro-forceps and ultrasound-blasters. The equipment of Renaissance anatomists and physicians was more like that of a butcher or chef. The tools fulfilled few major functions, such as sawing, slicing, gripping, and easing the tissues apart. However, body parts range from large, tough bones and joints to fragile, tiny nerves and vessels, so these 19th-century dissecting tools were graded in a range of sizes and penetrating power.

Instruments illustrated by Vesalius in the second edition of his book, 1555

Serrated saw blade

Large bone saw

Wooden handle for minimum slip and maximum grip

Tensioning screw to tighten blade

Contoured end to fit palm of hand

11

The microscopic body

I<small>N</small> 1609 I<small>TALIAN SCIENTIST</small> G<small>ALILEO</small> G<small>ALILEI</small> heard about the telescope, a new invention from The Netherlands. He copied it, and revolutionized people's ideas about the Sun and Moon, the stars and planets, and the Earth's place in outer space. By 1600 the early microscopes of Hans Jansen and his son, Zacharius, also in The Netherlands, were seen. Another great Italian scientist Marcello Malpighi soon used the invention, to look at "inner space" – the tiny structures inside plants and animals. The era of microbiology had begun. Soon microanatomists realized that all living things are made up of much smaller units. Even liquid blood contains minute rounded particles. In 1665 the term "cells" was applied to these units, in the book *Micrographia* by English scientist and founder of the Royal Society, Robert Hooke (1635-1703). Hooke had seen the microscopic box-like compartments in cork plant stems, which he likened to the rooms, or cells, of monks in their monastery. The name stuck, and today the cell is regarded as the basic building block of all living things, including the human body.

PIONEER MICROSCOPIST
Marcello Malpighi (1628-94) was one of the first and the greatest of microanatomists. He studied mainly at Bologna, where he identified many new microscopic parts of both human and animal bodies. His *De Viscerum Structura* (1659) described the glomerulus filtering units (p. 38) in the kidney, which are also known as malpighian corpuscles. He also saw blood capillaries connecting arteries and veins in the lungs, supporting William Harvey's ideas on blood circulation (p. 30).

WIDE-RANGING OBSERVER
Antoni van Leeuwenhoek (1632-1723) was a Dutch textile businessman who developed a spare-time hobby as self-taught scientist and microscopist. With his remarkable home-made microscopes he was among the first to study human blood cells (1674), the microanatomy of plants, insect eyes, the life cycles of fleas and aphids, microbes such as bacteria, and sperm cells. London's Royal Society published many of his descriptions, and he was eventually elected a fellow of the Society.

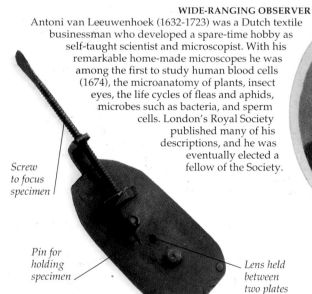

Screw to focus specimen

Pin for holding specimen

Lens held between two plates

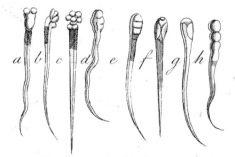

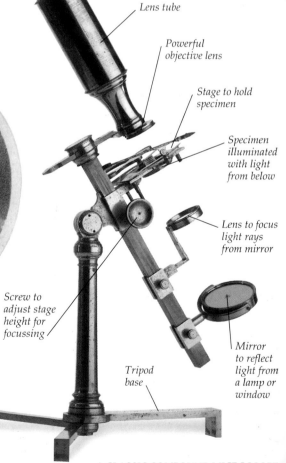

Eyepiece lens

Lens tube

Powerful objective lens

Stage to hold specimen

Specimen illuminated with light from below

Lens to focus light rays from mirror

Screw to adjust stage height for focussing

Tripod base

Mirror to reflect light from a lamp or window

HOME-GROUND LENSES
Most microscopes at the time of van Leeuwenhoek had two lenses, as shown on the right. His versions, life size above, had one tiny lens, which he ground and polished himself. His lenses were so accurate that the view was amazingly sharp and clear, and magnified up to 275 times life size. Van Leeuwenhoek's achievements helped to establish microscopy as a branch of science. He made about 400 microscopes in all, although no one knew how he lit the specimens brightly enough to see such immense detail.

a b c d e f g h

Van Leeuwenhoek's drawings of human sperm cells

A CLASSIC COMPOUND MICROSCOPE
Van Leeuwenhoek's microscopes were "simple", that is, having only one lens. Today, most microscopes are compound, using two or more lenses. This 19th-century model has all the basic features found on a modern microscope. In some models, the lens tube moves up and down to focus and give a sharp view; in others, the specimen stage moves. The specimen must be sliced thin enough for light to be transmitted through it, from the mirror below, up through the lenses to the eye. So this type of microscope is known as a transmission light microscope.

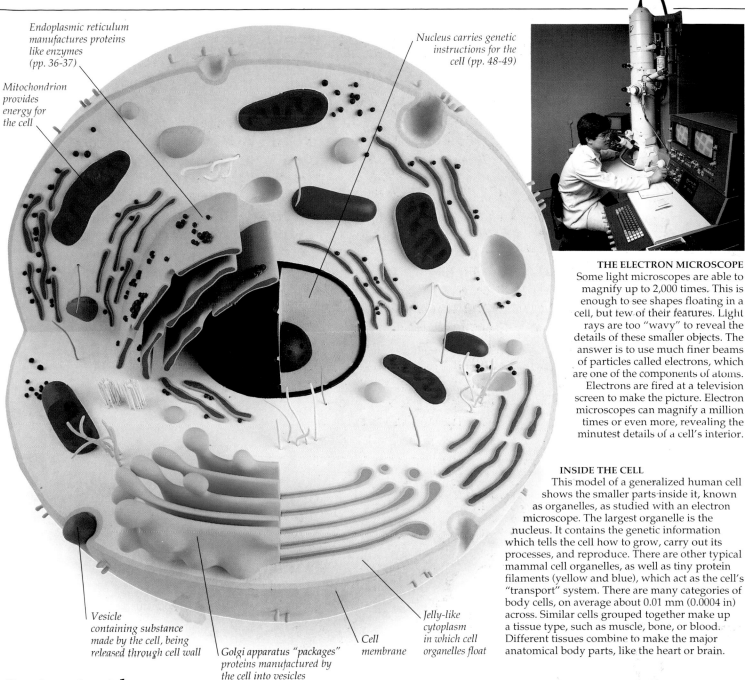

Endoplasmic reticulum manufactures proteins like enzymes (pp. 36-37)

Mitochondrion provides energy for the cell

Nucleus carries genetic instructions for the cell (pp. 48-49)

Vesicle containing substance made by the cell, being released through cell wall

Golgi apparatus "packages" proteins manufactured by the cell into vesicles

Cell membrane

Jelly-like cytoplasm in which cell organelles float

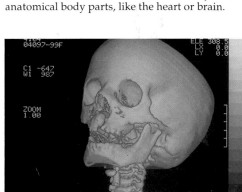

THE ELECTRON MICROSCOPE

Some light microscopes are able to magnify up to 2,000 times. This is enough to see shapes floating in a cell, but few of their features. Light rays are too "wavy" to reveal the details of these smaller objects. The answer is to use much finer beams of particles called electrons, which are one of the components of atoms. Electrons are fired at a television screen to make the picture. Electron microscopes can magnify a million times or even more, revealing the minutest details of a cell's interior.

INSIDE THE CELL

This model of a generalized human cell shows the smaller parts inside it, known as organelles, as studied with an electron microscope. The largest organelle is the nucleus. It contains the genetic information which tells the cell how to grow, carry out its processes, and reproduce. There are other typical mammal cell organelles, as well as tiny protein filaments (yellow and blue), which act as the cell's "transport" system. There are many categories of body cells, on average about 0.01 mm (0.0004 in) across. Similar cells grouped together make up a tissue type, such as muscle, bone, or blood. Different tissues combine to make the major anatomical body parts, like the heart or brain.

Seeing inside

Until the early 20th century, the only way to look inside the body was to cut it open. X-rays were discovered in 1895 by Wilhelm Roentgen (1845-1923), the German scientist. These pass through most soft body tissues such as muscles, but less easily through hard parts such as bone. Shining X-rays through a body part on to a special photographic plate produces an image of the bones inside. X-rays were soon being used to detect broken bones. This specialist area of medicine is called radiology.

MYSTERIOUS RAYS

Roentgen discovered rays that made certain chemicals glow and fogged photographic paper. He called them X-rays because he did not know their nature. His work intrigued many scientists at the time, one of whom was Marie Curie (1867-1934), left, who continued his line of research. She studied radioactivity, and in 1898 she identified radium. Marie Curie also worked on the application of X-rays for medical diagnosis.

IMAGING TODAY

It is now known that high levels of X-rays and radioactivity can damage living tissues, so modern X-ray imaging machines use very low levels. The computerized tomography, or CT, scanner beams tiny amounts of X-rays at various angles through the body, building up a picture, slice by slice. A computer combines the two-dimensional results, to build a three-dimensional image, such as this skull.

The body's framework

WHEN A HUMAN BODY REACHES THE END of its life, the flesh soon rots away. Left behind is a set of stiff, pale objects which provided an inner framework, supporting and protecting the softer tissues around them. The framework is the skeleton, made up of 206 bones. Early people must have wondered at these, and why they persist so long after death. Indeed, these people used animal and human bones as symbols of power and victory, for carvings, and as tools and ornaments. Because of their toughness and durability, bones could be studied in detail and they regularly found their way into medical textbooks. The great Galen of Ancient Rome wrote *Bones for Beginners* 1,800 years ago, and introduced some of the technical terms still in use today. From the times of Ancient Rome until the Renaissance, physicians were generally forbidden by religion or tradition from looking inside human corpses. However, after a few weeks of vultures and maggots, the bones were exposed, and study could proceed.

SYMBOL OF DEATH
Skeletons are enduring symbols of danger, disease, death, and destruction – from this 15th-century *Dance of Death* drawing, to a pirate's skull-and-crossbones. In medieval times the picked-clean skeletons of gallows victims were left swaying in the breeze on the hangman's noose, as a warning to others.

LOOKING AT BONES
For centuries, bones were regarded as lifeless, inactive supporters of the active softer parts around them. Gradually anatomists saw that bones were very much alive, with their own blood vessels and nerves (pp. 16-17). The idea was developed that bones were rigid, yet busy centres for the tissues around them. This lesson in skeletal anatomy is from a manuscript by surgeon Guy de Chauliac, in 1363.

STRUTS AND LEVERS
The skeleton has evolved on sound mechanical principles. For example, each arm has two sets of long bones that can extend the reach of the hand, or fold back on themselves. These principles have been copied by engineers, designing objects from cranes to adjustable desk lamps.

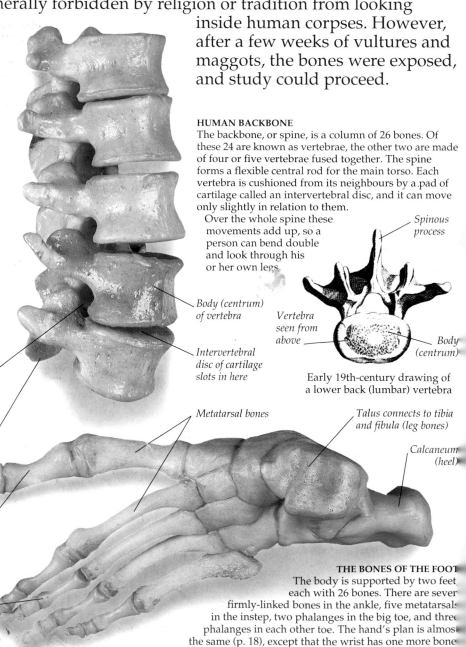

HUMAN BACKBONE
The backbone, or spine, is a column of 26 bones. Of these 24 are known as vertebrae, the other two are made of four or five vertebrae fused together. The spine forms a flexible central rod for the main torso. Each vertebra is cushioned from its neighbours by a pad of cartilage called an intervertebral disc, and it can move only slightly in relation to them.

Over the whole spine these movements add up, so a person can bend double and look through his or her own legs.

Spinous process

Vertebra seen from above

Body (centrum)

Early 19th-century drawing of a lower back (lumbar) vertebra

Spinal cord nerves (pp. 58-59) are protected by vertebrae

Spinous process, or bump, makes the backbone knobbly to the touch

Body (centrum) of vertebra

Intervertebral disc of cartilage slots in here

Metatarsal bones

Talus connects to tibia and fibula (leg bones)

Calcaneum (heel)

Big toe has only two phalanges

Smaller toes each have three phalanges

THE BONES OF THE FOOT
The body is supported by two feet, each with 26 bones. There are seven firmly-linked bones in the ankle, five metatarsals in the instep, two phalanges in the big toe, and three phalanges in each other toe. The hand's plan is almost the same (p. 18), except that the wrist has one more bone.

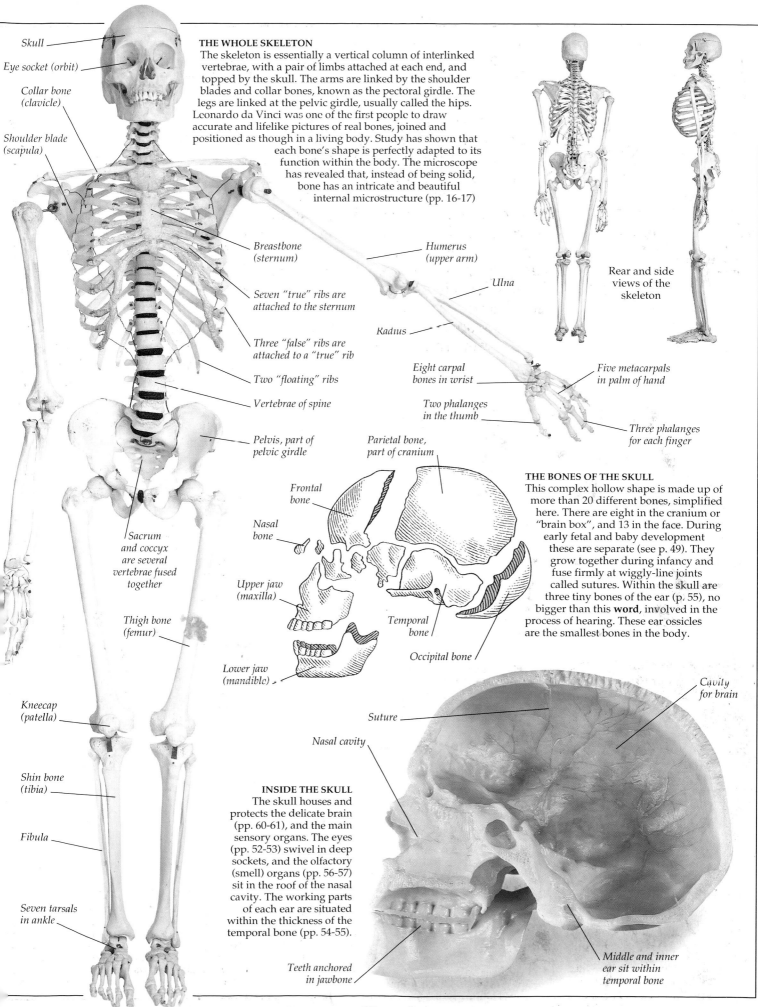

Skull

Eye socket (orbit)

Collar bone (clavicle)

Shoulder blade (scapula)

THE WHOLE SKELETON

The skeleton is essentially a vertical column of interlinked vertebrae, with a pair of limbs attached at each end, and topped by the skull. The arms are linked by the shoulder blades and collar bones, known as the pectoral girdle. The legs are linked at the pelvic girdle, usually called the hips. Leonardo da Vinci was one of the first people to draw accurate and lifelike pictures of real bones, joined and positioned as though in a living body. Study has shown that each bone's shape is perfectly adapted to its function within the body. The microscope has revealed that, instead of being solid, bone has an intricate and beautiful internal microstructure (pp. 16-17)

Rear and side views of the skeleton

Breastbone (sternum)

Humerus (upper arm)

Ulna

Seven "true" ribs are attached to the sternum

Radius

Three "false" ribs are attached to a "true" rib

Two "floating" ribs

Vertebrae of spine

Eight carpal bones in wrist

Five metacarpals in palm of hand

Two phalanges in the thumb

Three phalanges for each finger

Pelvis, part of pelvic girdle

Parietal bone, part of cranium

Sacrum and coccyx are several vertebrae fused together

Frontal bone

Nasal bone

THE BONES OF THE SKULL

This complex hollow shape is made up of more than 20 different bones, simplified here. There are eight in the cranium or "brain box", and 13 in the face. During early fetal and baby development these are separate (see p. 49). They grow together during infancy and fuse firmly at wiggly-line joints called sutures. Within the skull are three tiny bones of the ear (p. 55), no bigger than this **word**, involved in the process of hearing. These ear ossicles are the smallest bones in the body.

Upper jaw (maxilla)

Thigh bone (femur)

Temporal bone

Occipital bone

Lower jaw (mandible)

Cavity for brain

Suture

Nasal cavity

Kneecap (patella)

Shin bone (tibia)

Fibula

INSIDE THE SKULL

The skull houses and protects the delicate brain (pp. 60-61), and the main sensory organs. The eyes (pp. 52-53) swivel in deep sockets, and the olfactory (smell) organs (pp. 56-57) sit in the roof of the nasal cavity. The working parts of each ear are situated within the thickness of the temporal bone (pp. 54-55).

Seven tarsals in ankle

Teeth anchored in jawbone

Middle and inner ear sit within temporal bone

Inside bones

BONES ARE MOST OFTEN SEEN as pale, dry, flaky objects in museums, or lying in the countryside as the last remnants of a dead animal. They might not seem very interesting, but they do have a life of their own. Our prehistoric ancestors would have had a more intimate knowledge of bones than people today. More than a million years ago, early humans used rock axes and stone hammers to crack open animal bones, presumably to get at the nutritious marrow inside. They would see that a typical bone has a tough skin that we call the periosteum, covering an outer shell of compact bone, which is hard and dense. The compact bone encloses an inner layer of lighter, honeycombed cancellous or spongy bone, with soft marrow at the centre. When early microscopists peered at thin slices of bone, they were amazed to see a complex and regular micro-architecture, which reflects bone's active life. The structural unit of compact bone is the tube-shaped Haversian system, named after English physician Clopton Havers (1650-1701). He published his observations in 1691, and opened the way for the research of later physiologists, who found that bones had many roles, in addition to holding up the body.

GROWING BONE
In the early embryo (p. 44), the body does not have bones. Their shapes begin as a softer substance, cartilage, or gristle. Nuggets of bone, known as ossification centres, then develop at certain points within the cartilage. They grow and spread, turning the cartilage into true bone. In this unborn baby's hand, speckled areas of bone are replacing the clear areas of cartilage.

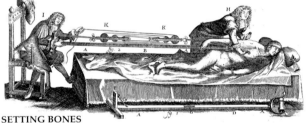

SETTING BONES
Fossilized human skeletons 100,000 years old show that broken bones were repositioned, to heal better. Bone setting is an ancient art. Here a late 17th-century rope-and-pulley invention is pulling broken arm bone back into place.

INSIDE THE HIP
In the hip joint, the ball-shaped head of the femur (thigh bone) fits into a cup-shaped socket in the pelvis (hip bone). The head of the femur is mainly cancellous or spongy bone, surrounded by a thin shell of dense compact bone. Engineers have analyzed the stresses and strains on bones such as this, and constructed mechanical models. They find that compact bone develops where needed, in the areas of most stress. Cancellous bone is a "filler". It is not so strong, but it is lighter and less of a drain on the body's mineral supplies.

SPONGY BONE
This microscopic view of cancellous, or spongy, bone shows its open system of bony lattices and struts, known as trabeculae. In living bone the spaces are filled with body fluids and wandering cells (p. 13). Landing from an energetic leap, muscles exert tremendous pressure in the hip and knee joints, so the bone must stand compression (squeezing) forces of up to half a tonne (0.45 tons).

Head of femur

Spongy bone

Compact bone

Central cavity for marrow

Muscle tissue

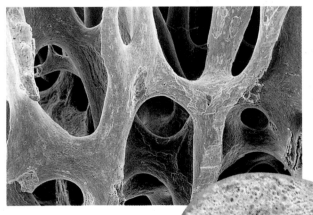

BONES AS TUBES
Engineers have long known that weight-for-strength there are few structural shapes to rival the tube. This cutaway humerus from the upper arm shows how the main shaft is a narrow tube, while the ends are expanded to spread the pressure in their joints with adjacent bones.

Head of humerus

Neck of humerus

Spongy bone where less strength is needed

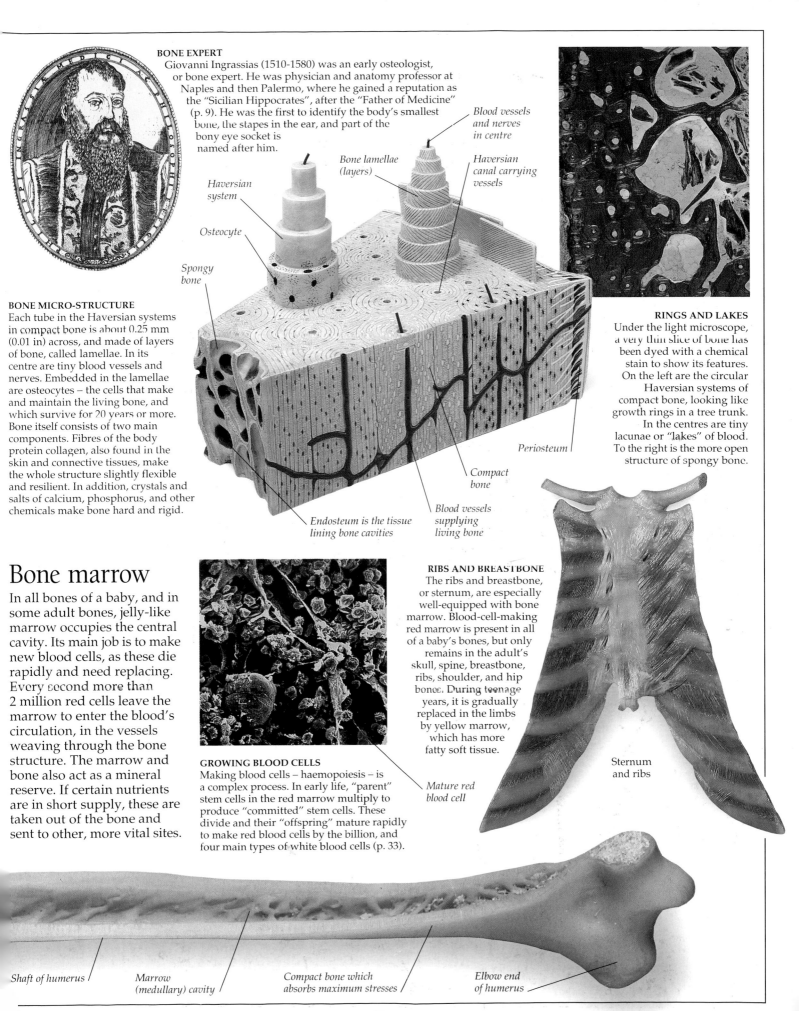

BONE EXPERT
Giovanni Ingrassias (1510-1580) was an early osteologist, or bone expert. He was physician and anatomy professor at Naples and then Palermo, where he gained a reputation as the "Sicilian Hippocrates", after the "Father of Medicine" (p. 9). He was the first to identify the body's smallest bone, the stapes in the ear, and part of the bony eye socket is named after him.

Blood vessels and nerves in centre

Bone lamellae (layers)

Haversian canal carrying vessels

Haversian system

Osteocyte

Spongy bone

BONE MICRO-STRUCTURE
Each tube in the Haversian systems in compact bone is about 0.25 mm (0.01 in) across, and made of layers of bone, called lamellae. In its centre are tiny blood vessels and nerves. Embedded in the lamellae are osteocytes – the cells that make and maintain the living bone, and which survive for 20 years or more. Bone itself consists of two main components. Fibres of the body protein collagen, also found in the skin and connective tissues, make the whole structure slightly flexible and resilient. In addition, crystals and salts of calcium, phosphorus, and other chemicals make bone hard and rigid.

Endosteum is the tissue lining bone cavities

Compact bone

Blood vessels supplying living bone

Periosteum

RINGS AND LAKES
Under the light microscope, a very thin slice of bone has been dyed with a chemical stain to show its features. On the left are the circular Haversian systems of compact bone, looking like growth rings in a tree trunk. In the centres are tiny lacunae or "lakes" of blood. To the right is the more open structure of spongy bone.

Bone marrow

In all bones of a baby, and in some adult bones, jelly-like marrow occupies the central cavity. Its main job is to make new blood cells, as these die rapidly and need replacing. Every second more than 2 million red cells leave the marrow to enter the blood's circulation, in the vessels weaving through the bone structure. The marrow and bone also act as a mineral reserve. If certain nutrients are in short supply, these are taken out of the bone and sent to other, more vital sites.

GROWING BLOOD CELLS
Making blood cells – haemopoiesis – is a complex process. In early life, "parent" stem cells in the red marrow multiply to produce "committed" stem cells. These divide and their "offspring" mature rapidly to make red blood cells by the billion, and four main types of white blood cells (p. 33).

Mature red blood cell

RIBS AND BREASTBONE
The ribs and breastbone, or sternum, are especially well-equipped with bone marrow. Blood-cell-making red marrow is present in all of a baby's bones, but only remains in the adult's skull, spine, breastbone, ribs, shoulder, and hip bones. During teenage years, it is gradually replaced in the limbs by yellow marrow, which has more fatty soft tissue.

Sternum and ribs

Shaft of humerus

Marrow (medullary) cavity

Compact bone which absorbs maximum stresses

Elbow end of humerus

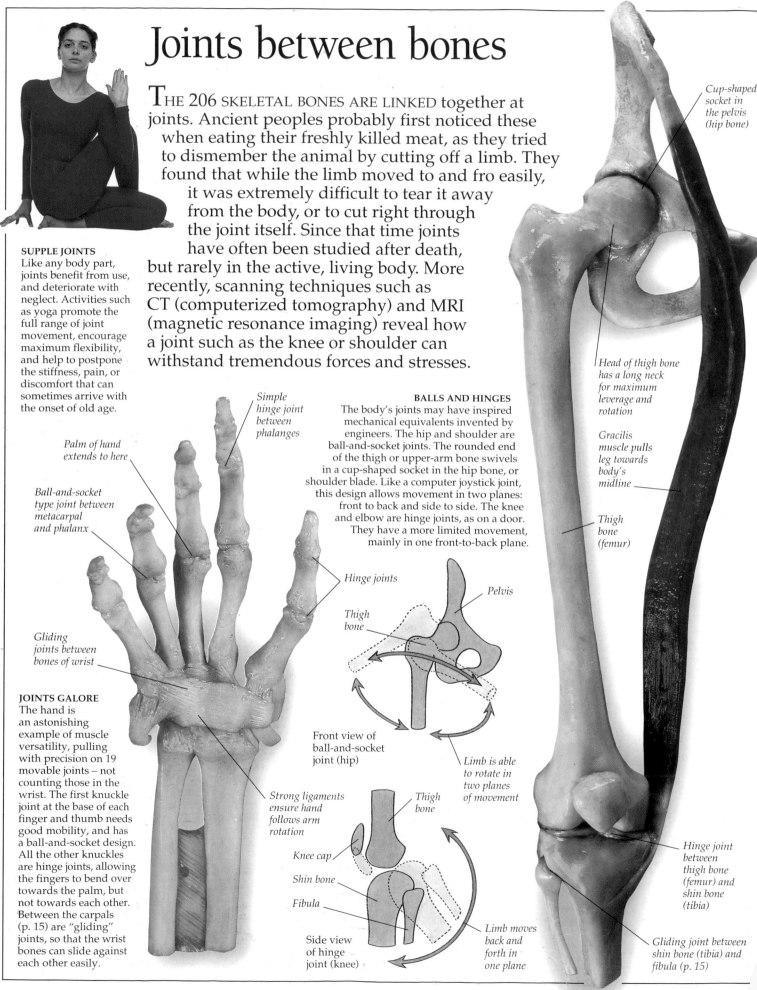

Joints between bones

The 206 skeletal bones are linked together at joints. Ancient peoples probably first noticed these when eating their freshly killed meat, as they tried to dismember the animal by cutting off a limb. They found that while the limb moved to and fro easily, it was extremely difficult to tear it away from the body, or to cut right through the joint itself. Since that time joints have often been studied after death, but rarely in the active, living body. More recently, scanning techniques such as CT (computerized tomography) and MRI (magnetic resonance imaging) reveal how a joint such as the knee or shoulder can withstand tremendous forces and stresses.

SUPPLE JOINTS
Like any body part, joints benefit from use, and deteriorate with neglect. Activities such as yoga promote the full range of joint movement, encourage maximum flexibility, and help to postpone the stiffness, pain, or discomfort that can sometimes arrive with the onset of old age.

JOINTS GALORE
The hand is an astonishing example of muscle versatility, pulling with precision on 19 movable joints – not counting those in the wrist. The first knuckle joint at the base of each finger and thumb needs good mobility, and has a ball-and-socket design. All the other knuckles are hinge joints, allowing the fingers to bend over towards the palm, but not towards each other. Between the carpals (p. 15) are "gliding" joints, so that the wrist bones can slide against each other easily.

BALLS AND HINGES
The body's joints may have inspired mechanical equivalents invented by engineers. The hip and shoulder are ball-and-socket joints. The rounded end of the thigh or upper-arm bone swivels in a cup-shaped socket in the hip bone, or shoulder blade. Like a computer joystick joint, this design allows movement in two planes: front to back and side to side. The knee and elbow are hinge joints, as on a door. They have a more limited movement, mainly in one front-to-back plane.

Simple hinge joint between phalanges

Palm of hand extends to here

Ball-and-socket type joint between metacarpal and phalanx

Gliding joints between bones of wrist

Hinge joints

Strong ligaments ensure hand follows arm rotation

Pelvis

Thigh bone

Front view of ball-and-socket joint (hip)

Limb is able to rotate in two planes of movement

Thigh bone

Knee cap

Shin bone

Fibula

Side view of hinge joint (knee)

Limb moves back and forth in one plane

Cup-shaped socket in the pelvis (hip bone)

Head of thigh bone has a long neck for maximum leverage and rotation

Gracilis muscle pulls leg towards body's midline

Thigh bone (femur)

Hinge joint between thigh bone (femur) and shin bone (tibia)

Gliding joint between shin bone (tibia) and fibula (p. 15)

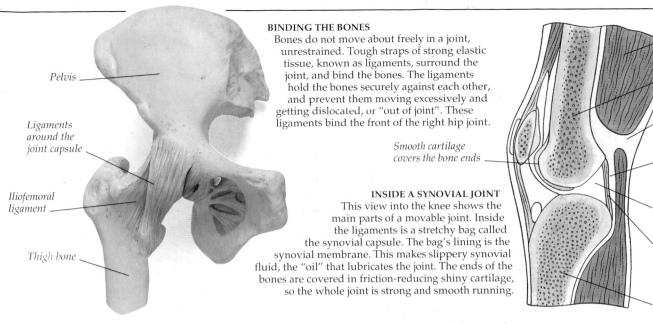

BINDING THE BONES
Bones do not move about freely in a joint, unrestrained. Tough straps of strong elastic tissue, known as ligaments, surround the joint, and bind the bones. The ligaments hold the bones securely against each other, and prevent them moving excessively and getting dislocated, or "out of joint". These ligaments bind the front of the right hip joint.

Pelvis

Ligaments around the joint capsule

Iliofemoral ligament

Thigh bone

Muscle

Thigh bone

Fatty tissue

Ligaments bind the bones

Synovial fluid (clear)

Synovial membrane lines capsule

Shin bone

Smooth cartilage covers the bone ends

INSIDE A SYNOVIAL JOINT
This view into the knee shows the main parts of a movable joint. Inside the ligaments is a stretchy bag called the synovial capsule. The bag's lining is the synovial membrane. This makes slippery synovial fluid, the "oil" that lubricates the joint. The ends of the bones are covered in friction-reducing shiny cartilage, so the whole joint is strong and smooth running.

Cartilage

There are several types of cartilage, or "gristle", in the body. The main type is hyaline cartilage. It is pearly light blue and makes up structural parts such as the nose, voicebox, windpipe, and lung airways (pp. 24-25). Inside a joint, a specialized hyaline cartilage, called articular hyaline cartilage, covers the ends of bones where they press and rub against each other. It is glossy to reduce friction, and slightly squashy to absorb jolts. Another type is white fibrocartilage, which is found in discs in between the vertebrae (p. 14) and in parts of certain joints, such as the sockets in the shoulder and hip bones, to withstand the immense wear. A third type found in parts of the ears and the larynx, is springy and elastic, and is called yellow fibrocartilage.

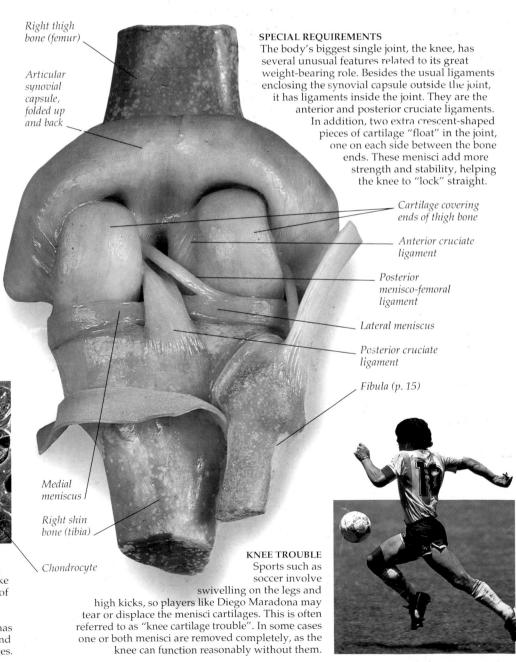

Right thigh bone (femur)

Articular synovial capsule, folded up and back

SPECIAL REQUIREMENTS
The body's biggest single joint, the knee, has several unusual features related to its great weight-bearing role. Besides the usual ligaments enclosing the synovial capsule outside the joint, it has ligaments inside the joint. They are the anterior and posterior cruciate ligaments. In addition, two extra crescent-shaped pieces of cartilage "float" in the joint, one on each side between the bone ends. These menisci add more strength and stability, helping the knee to "lock" straight.

Cartilage covering ends of thigh bone

Anterior cruciate ligament

Posterior menisco-femoral ligament

Lateral meniscus

Posterior cruciate ligament

Fibula (p. 15)

Medial meniscus

Right shin bone (tibia)

Chondrocyte

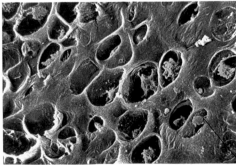

CARTILAGE CELLS
Cartilage-making cells are called chondrocytes. They live entombed in the matrix that they make around themselves. This is composed of fibres of the proteins collagen and elastin, woven into a stiff jelly with water, dissolved carbohydrates such as starches, and body minerals. Cartilage has a limited blood supply, and nutrients seep in and wastes seep out to blood vessels around the edges.

KNEE TROUBLE
Sports such as soccer involve swivelling on the legs and high kicks, so players like Diego Maradona may tear or displace the menisci cartilages. This is often referred to as "knee cartilage trouble". In some cases one or both menisci are removed completely, as the knee can function reasonably without them.

The body's muscles

A CHUNK OF JUICY MUSCLE is the predator's prime meal in the natural world, from a lion gnawing at a gazelle to a human eating a steak. On average most animals, including humans, are one-half muscle. Muscles are the body's movers. This is because a muscle is a lump of tissue specialized to do a simple job: to shorten, or contract. Every movement, from the blink of an eye to sprinting a race, is driven by the body's muscular system. Muscles, along with the bones they pull, were among the first parts of the body to be drawn, described and named, because of the general interest in the body's movement – and eating meat. Galen of Ancient Rome identified about 300 individual skeletal muscles, just under half the body's total. Leonardo da Vinci noted and named more, and his extraordinary engravings and paintings of living people reflected this knowledge in the supple bulges and curves under their skin. The volume, *Epitome*, of Andreas Vesalius' monumental work *De Fabrica* (1543) is a classic of science and art, depicting yet more muscles in carefully dissected and posed bodies.

ROCKS AND MUSCLES
Danish scientist Niels Stensen (1638-1686), was a student at Copenhagen, Amsterdam, and Leiden. He carried out microscopic work on muscles and realized that their contraction was due to the combined shortening of the thousands of tiny, thin fibres that make up each whole muscle. Besides his five books on anatomy, he was a crystal expert, and the "father" of geology.

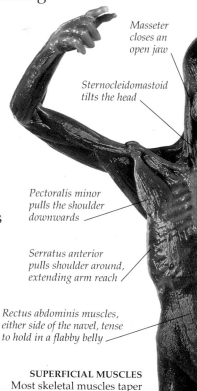

Masseter closes an open jaw

Sternocleidomastoid tilts the head

Pectoralis major pulls the arm in and rotates it

Deltoid raises and twists the upper arm

Connective tissue adheres to muscle layer beneath skin

Pectoralis minor pulls the shoulder downwards

Biceps brachii bends the elbow

Serratus anterior pulls shoulder around, extending arm reach

Flexors bend the fingers

Rectus abdominis muscles, either side of the navel, tense to hold in a flabby belly

SUPERFICIAL MUSCLES
Most skeletal muscles taper at their ends into rope-like tendons. These are anchored strongly on to bones or other muscles. The body has over 640 skeletal muscles, arranged layer on layer, criss-crossing and overlapping, so that each bone may be pulled in almost any direction. The muscles that are visible when the skin and underlying fat are removed, are termed superficial muscles.

Sartorius twists thigh, and bends hip and knee

Quadriceps femoris is made up of four smaller muscles

Tibialis anterior raises the foot

Extensor muscles raise ball of foot and curl toes upward

Superficial muscles, front view

THE ULTIMATE BOOK
Italian anatomist and teacher Giorgio Baglivi (1668-1707) told his students: "You will never find a more interesting, more instructive book than the patient himself". He had an over-simple belief that the body was a set of small machines, regarding the blood vessels as a system of water pipes and the lungs as bellows. However, he was the first to note that skeletal muscles, which pull on bones, are different from muscles working the intestines and other organs. Under the microscope, skeletal muscles look striped while gut muscles do not.

Smooth muscle in the gut walls

Cardiac muscle

THREE TYPES OF MUSCLE
The body's three types of muscle have a variety of names. One type is called skeletal muscle, because it moves the skeleton's bones; it is also called striped or striated muscle (see drawing, top right), since under the microscope it has a striped appearance, and voluntary muscle, as it responds to the brain's conscious will. Visceral muscle in the intestines and abdominal organs is called smooth muscle, because it lacks stripes, and involuntary muscle, as it works without conscious involvement. The third type is cardiac muscle or myocardium, found solely in the heart.

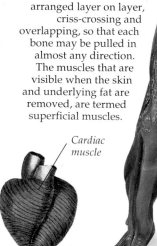

18th-century drawings of the heart and gut

MR MUSCLE

Bodybuilders take pride in developing, emphasizing and flexing their muscles. Many of the body's superficial muscles can be identified, beautifully defined, rippling just below their skin. When a muscle is tensed and shortened, its main body, or belly, bulges and becomes wider.

INSIDE A MUSCLE

Each skeletal muscle is wrapped in a tough sheath, the epimysium. Within are bundles of hair-like muscle fibres, each wrapped in their own sheath, the perimysium. The fibres are giant multi-cells, some more than 10 mm (0.4 in) long, containing several nuclei and huge numbers of mitochondria (pp. 12-13). In turn, one fibre is a bundle of fibrils, the contracting units (p. 22). Muscle has a rich blood supply, bringing energy for contraction, and nerves that instruct which fibres to contract, and when.

Epimysium

Bundle of muscle fibres

Muscle fibre

Motor nerve cell (pp. 58-59)

Perimysium

Striped fibril

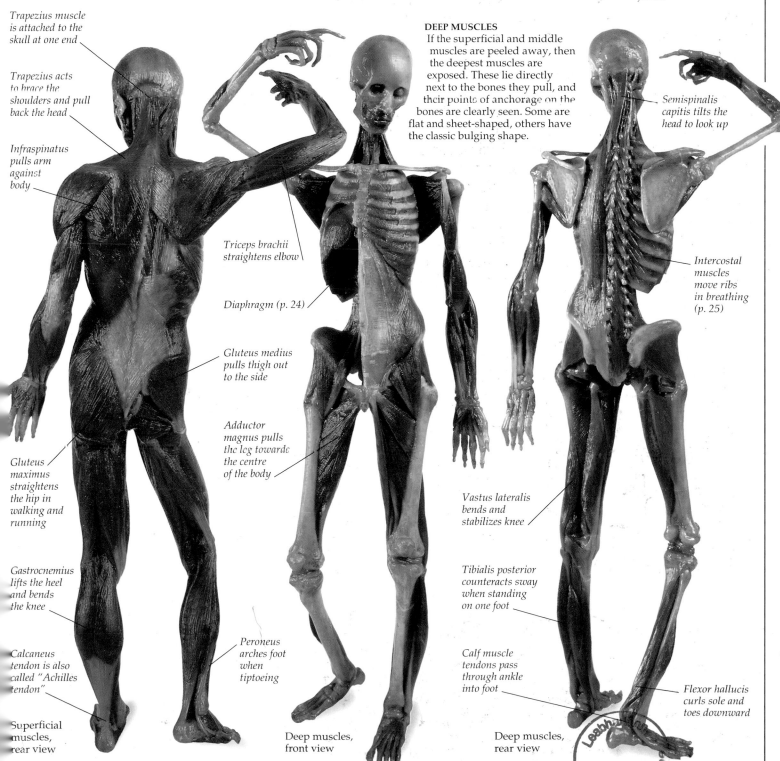

Trapezius muscle is attached to the skull at one end

Trapezius acts to brace the shoulders and pull back the head

Infraspinatus pulls arm against body

DEEP MUSCLES

If the superficial and middle muscles are peeled away, then the deepest muscles are exposed. These lie directly next to the bones they pull, and their points of anchorage on the bones are clearly seen. Some are flat and sheet-shaped, others have the classic bulging shape.

Semispinalis capitis tilts the head to look up

Triceps brachii straightens elbow

Diaphragm (p. 24)

Gluteus medius pulls thigh out to the side

Intercostal muscles move ribs in breathing (p. 25)

Adductor magnus pulls the leg towards the centre of the body

Gluteus maximus straightens the hip in walking and running

Vastus lateralis bends and stabilizes knee

Tibialis posterior counteracts sway when standing on one foot

Gastrocnemius lifts the heel and bends the knee

Peroneus arches foot when tiptoeing

Calf muscle tendons pass through ankle into foot

Calcaneus tendon is also called "Achilles tendon"

Flexor hallucis curls sole and toes downward

Superficial muscles, rear view

Deep muscles, front view

Deep muscles, rear view

The moving body

By THE LATE 18TH CENTURY, virtually all of the body's muscles had been identified and named. They are invariably in mirror-image pairs, emphasizing the symmetrical nature of the skeleton, as opposed to the inner organs such as the intestines. The biggest muscle is the gluteus maximus (p. 21) in the buttock. The smallest muscle is the stapedius, attached to the smallest bone, the stapes or stirrup (p. 55), inside the ear. Like a short piece of cotton thread, it pulls on the stapes to dampen the vibrations from too-loud sounds, preventing them from causing damage to the delicate inner ear. Once general muscle anatomy was complete, the microscopists and physiologists then discovered exactly how muscles work. Jan Swammerdam (1637-1680) showed that muscles alter in shape, not in size, during contraction. Luigi Galvani (1737-1798) (p. 58) noted the link between muscles and electricity. Subsequent research showed that muscles contract on stimulation by the tiny electrical impulses of nerve signals.

THE THREE "S" WORDS
Muscle fitness can be assessed by three s-words: strength, stamina, and suppleness. Some pursuits develop only one factor, but moving activities like dancing and swimming promote all three factors.

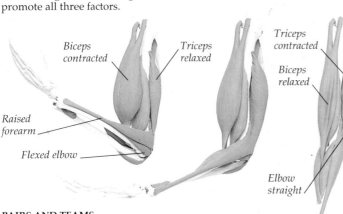

Biceps contracted

Triceps relaxed

Triceps contracted

Biceps relaxed

Raised forearm

Flexed elbow

Elbow straight

PAIRS AND TEAMS
Muscles can only contract and pull. They cannot forcibly lengthen and push, so many are arranged in opposing pairs. For example, the biceps brachii in the upper arm pulls the forearm bones and bends the elbow. Its opposing partner, the triceps, pulls the forearm bones the other way and so straightens the elbow. In practice, most body movements result from carefully controlled contractions of several muscles, working in teams.

MOVING THE ARM AND HAND
Muscles in the upper chest and back move the shoulder; those in the upper arm move the elbow; those in the forearm move the wrist and fingers. The leg has a very similar overall design. Traditionally, anatomists call the relatively "fixed" end of the muscle, nearest the centre of the body, the origin of the muscle, and the farther end, which "moves", the insertion.

Brachioradialis bends the elbow rapidly

Tendon of flexor carpi radialis which bends (flexes) the wrist

Palmar aponeurosis of fibrous tissue (p. 51)

Artery supplying energy-rich blood to limb (pp. 32-33)

Pronator teres twists the forearm inwards

Carpal tunnel

FIBRIL CONTRACTION
Under the electron microscope, a thin slice of fibrils (p. 21) from skeletal muscle reveals their stripy bands. These are made of rows and rows of two protein filaments, actin (yellow lines) and myosin (brown lines). When a muscle contracts the actin filaments slide ratchet-like past the myosin filaments, bringing the bands closer together and shortening (and fattening) the muscle. The blue, bubble-like structure is called the sarcoplasmic reticulum, and it transmits nerve impulses to the fibrils.

Large deltoid muscle
lifts the entire limb

Jugular
vein

Vein takes "stale" blood
back towards the heart

Coracobrachialis
pulls the arm
towards the body

MOVING THE WRIST AND FINGERS
Slim flexor digitorum muscles on the
inside of the forearm have long tendons
which run through a "watch strap" of
ligament fibres, known as the carpal
tunnel, in the wrist. These muscles
flex the fingers, bending their
tips towards the palm, as when
playing the piano, or
making a gripping fist.

Biceps brachii
bends elbow
and twists
wrist

Part of serratus
anterior, which
helps arm to reach out

Ribs (p. 15)

Nerves give instructions
to the muscles from the
brain (pp. 58-59)

Procerus
wrinkles bridge
of nose to frown

Intercostal
muscles raise the
ribs in breathing

Branches of
facial nerve

Levator labii superior
lifts and curls upper
lip to pucker

THE HEAD AND NECK
The head weighs
about 4 kg (8.8 lb).
To balance and move
this heavy load on the
topmost bones of the spine,
numerous muscles attach
the base of the skull to the
vertebrae, shoulder blades, and
other bones in the upper chest
(pp. 14-15). About 30 muscles
produce a galaxy of facial
expressions, allowing people
to communicate silently.
Many of these muscles
are not attached to bones,
but to their fellow muscles.
About 10 muscles meet near the
corner of the mouth, anchored to
a disc of fibrous tissue known as
the modiolus. The eyelids and
lips contain circlets of muscle
that close when they contract.

Orbicularis oris
closes lips and
purses them

Modiolus
is at corner
of mouth

Mylohyoid forms
floor of mouth and
helps to swallow

Sternohyoid pulls
floor of mouth and
voice box down

Sternocleidomastoid
holds the head
steady and tilts it
up and sideways

Trapezius prevents the
head from falling forward

SWAMMERDAM OF AMSTERDAM
Jan Swammerdam (1637-1680) qualified as a doctor,
but spent most of his working life peering down a
microscope. He devised methods of making fresh
frog muscles contract by pinching the nerves
attached to them. By immersing the muscle in a
water-filled device, he showed for the first time that
when a muscle shortens its total volume does not
increase, as had long been believed, it stays the same.

Breathing to live

WHY DOES THE LIVING BODY DIE if it cannot breathe? Breathing has a history of mystery. Ancient Greeks such as Plato and Aristotle thought that food was burned in the heart as a "vital flame", which created life and warmth. Breathing cooled the flame, and prevented it from burning too high and consuming the body. There was not much progress on this view until William Harvey described the workings of the heart (pp. 28-29). Then tiny blood vessels and air sacs were discovered in the lungs. Scientists such as Robert Boyle, Robert Hooke, and John Mayow investigated breathing using chemistry, and the mechanical principles of the bellows and suction pump. It is now known that the lungs work like bellows to absorb oxygen. This is needed for a set of bodily chemical reactions in every cell, known as cellular respiration. This process "slow-burns" nutrients like sugars, to liberate energy for the cell's life processes. The body is unable to store oxygen, so it needs a continuous supply from the air, which is one-fifth oxygen.

USEFUL SIDE EFFECT
The body uses the airflow from breathing in several ways. One is to blow air into a confined space, to make the air and container vibrate. If that container is a wind instrument, like Charlie Parker's saxophone and Miles Davis' trumpet, it can produce inspiring sounds. Great breath control is needed, from chest muscles ruled by the musician's brain.

GALEN'S TEACHINGS
Influential Roman physician Claudius Galen enlarged on the breathing notions of the Greeks. He devised a complex theory of breathing based on several earlier writers. He thought that *pneuma*, a natural "world spirit", seeped from the air down the windpipe into the lungs, along hollow pulmonary veins and into the heart, where it added special life to the vital flame. This "vital spirit" was then distributed through the arterial system. The air picked up waste gases of combustion from the burning flame, and discharged them in the lungs.

BREATHING AND BURNING
English lawyer-turned-physician John Mayow (1640-1679) carried out many studies on breathing. He proved that the muscles of the chest and diaphragm made the lungs stretch and expand like sucking bellows, drawing in air. He also showed that breathing out was a non-muscular process, due to the lungs' natural elastic recoil. By putting animals and flames in sealed glass jars, singly and together, Mayow demonstrated that they used the same "fraction" of air, likening respiration to burning. The "fraction" was later identified and named as oxygen.

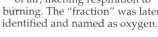

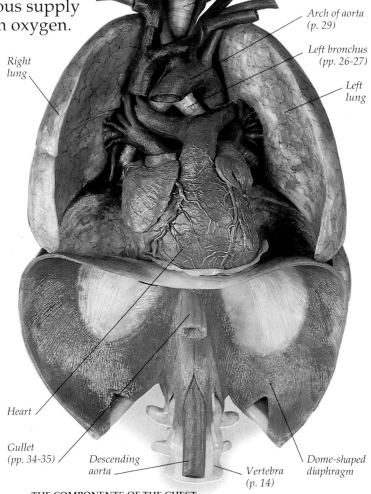

Epiglottis is a "safety" flap over the windpipe

Larynx

Windpipe (trachea) takes air to and from lungs

Arch of aorta (p. 29)

Left bronchus (pp. 26-27)

Left lung

Right lung

Heart

Gullet (pp. 34-35)

Descending aorta

Vertebra (p. 14)

Dome-shaped diaphragm

THE COMPONENTS OF THE CHEST
The chest is the upper of the torso's two major internal compartments, the lower being the abdomen. The dome-shaped diaphragm divides the two. Inside its flexible cage of vertebrae, ribs, and breastbone are those most vital of organs, the heart and lungs. The lungs absorb oxygen from breathed-in air into the blood, and the heart pumps this blood into the aorta, to distribute the oxygen throughout the body.

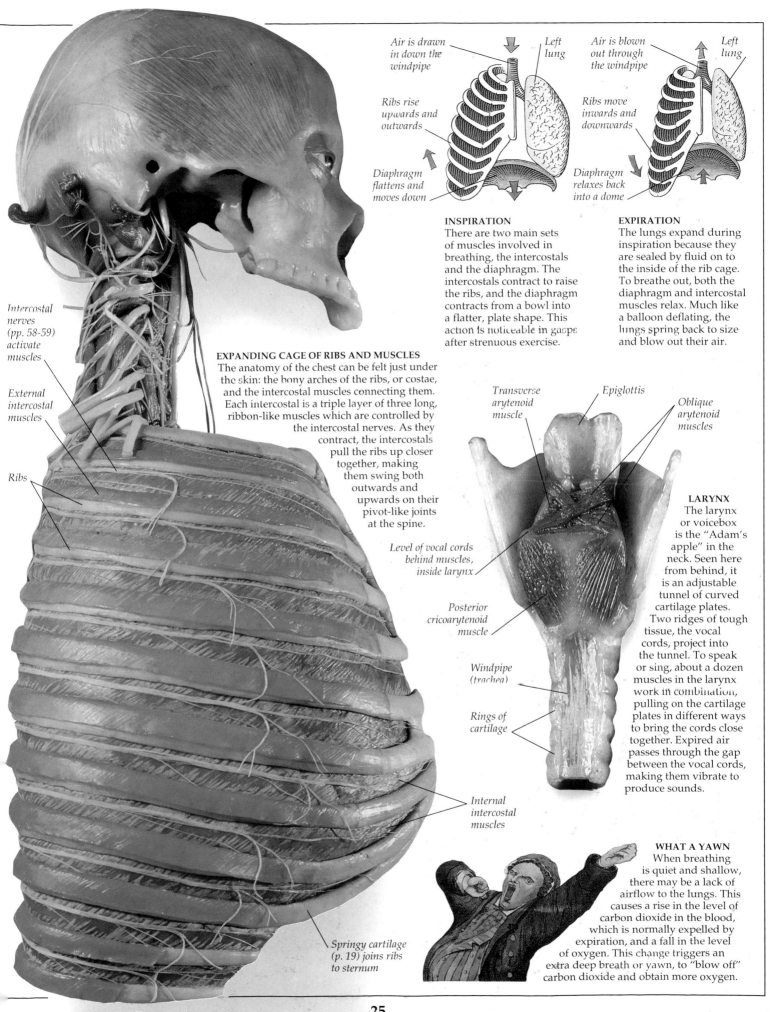

Air is drawn in down the windpipe

Left lung

Ribs rise upwards and outwards

Diaphragm flattens and moves down

Air is blown out through the windpipe

Left lung

Ribs move inwards and downwards

Diaphragm relaxes back into a dome

INSPIRATION
There are two main sets of muscles involved in breathing, the intercostals and the diaphragm. The intercostals contract to raise the ribs, and the diaphragm contracts from a bowl into a flatter, plate shape. This action is noticeable in gasps after strenuous exercise.

EXPIRATION
The lungs expand during inspiration because they are sealed by fluid on to the inside of the rib cage. To breathe out, both the diaphragm and intercostal muscles relax. Much like a balloon deflating, the lungs spring back to size and blow out their air.

Intercostal nerves (pp. 58-59) activate muscles

External intercostal muscles

Ribs

EXPANDING CAGE OF RIBS AND MUSCLES
The anatomy of the chest can be felt just under the skin: the bony arches of the ribs, or costae, and the intercostal muscles connecting them. Each intercostal is a triple layer of three long, ribbon-like muscles which are controlled by the intercostal nerves. As they contract, the intercostals pull the ribs up closer together, making them swing both outwards and upwards on their pivot-like joints at the spine.

Level of vocal cords behind muscles, inside larynx

Posterior cricoarytenoid muscle

Windpipe (trachea)

Rings of cartilage

Internal intercostal muscles

Springy cartilage (p. 19) joins ribs to sternum

Transverse arytenoid muscle

Epiglottis

Oblique arytenoid muscles

LARYNX
The larynx or voicebox is the "Adam's apple" in the neck. Seen here from behind, it is an adjustable tunnel of curved cartilage plates. Two ridges of tough tissue, the vocal cords, project into the tunnel. To speak or sing, about a dozen muscles in the larynx work in combination, pulling on the cartilage plates in different ways to bring the cords close together. Expired air passes through the gap between the vocal cords, making them vibrate to produce sounds.

WHAT A YAWN
When breathing is quiet and shallow, there may be a lack of airflow to the lungs. This causes a rise in the level of carbon dioxide in the blood, which is normally expelled by expiration, and a fall in the level of oxygen. This change triggers an extra deep breath or yawn, to "blow off" carbon dioxide and obtain more oxygen.

Inside the lungs

In 1777 French chemist Antoine Lavoisier finally identified the nature of the fraction of air that could support life and flames, and named it oxygen. "We can state in general that respiration is but a slow combustion . . . similar in all points to that taking place in a lamp or a burning candle. . . . In respiration as in combustion it is the atmospheric air which supplies the oxygen." Lavoisier used the term "respiration" for chemical reactions that take place within the body's cells. The word also means the physical processes of breathing. The nose, throat, windpipe, main airways and lungs, and the diaphragm are known as the respiratory system. By the time of Lavoisier, it was thought that the body used oxygen from air chemically to burn nutrients – but only in the lungs. Within 20 years Lazzaro Spallanzani showed that cellular respiration occurs in other tissues of the body. The lungs were gas-exchangers: they absorbed oxygen and gave off carbon dioxide. This agreed with discoveries about the blood circulation, and the finding that blood contains both oxygen and carbon dioxide.

OXYGEN NAMED
Antoine Lavoisier (1743-1794) carried out many chemistry experiments that were significant in the field of physiology, which he demonstrated to Parisian nobility. He named oxygen from Greek words meaning "acid-maker". Through his life he was involved in a variety of projects, including a plan for town lighting, explosives research, and the use of scientific methods in farming, as well as work for famine relief. He was guillotined in the aftermath of the French Revolution.

ALL-OVER RESPIRATION
Italian scientist Lazzaro Spallanzani (1729-1799) was in turn priest, lawyer, professor of logic and metaphysics, and professor of natural history at Pavia. He proposed that respiration did not happen just in the lungs, but in every tissue cell of the body. The blood was both oxygen distributor and the collector of carbon dioxide, pumped by the heart to all body tissues.

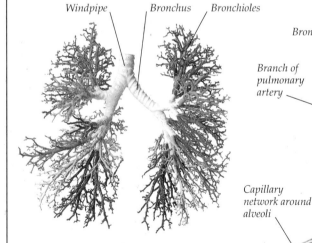

Windpipe *Bronchus* *Bronchioles*

Bronchiole

Branch of pulmonary artery

Branch of pulmonary vein

Terminal bronchiole

Capillary network around alveoli

Alveoli (air sacs)

Deoxygenated blood rich in carbon dioxide

Carbon dioxide passes into alveolus from blood

Stale air leaves alveolus

Fresh air enters

Oxygen diffuses from air in alveolus into blood

Freshly oxygenated blood

THE BRONCHIAL TREE
Inside the lungs is a branching, tree-like structure of air tubes, known as the bronchial tree. The windpipe divides into two large tubes known as bronchi, one to each lung. These split repeatedly, 15 or 20 times, forming thousands of terminal bronchioles, thinner than the finest hairs.

WHERE GAS EXCHANGE HAPPENS
Each terminal bronchiole ends at a bunch of bubble-like air sacs, called alveoli. There are about 350 million alveoli in each lung. They provide a tennis-court-sized area packed into the volume of the chest, to maximize gas exchange. Around each alveolus is a network of microscopic blood vessels, called capillaries.

REFRESHED WITH OXYGEN
The lining of each alveolus is incredibly thin, coated with a film of moisture in which gases can dissolve. Oxygen from the air inside seeps through the one-cell-thick wall of the capillary into the blood, turning its colour from dark to bright red. Carbon dioxide passes the opposite way.

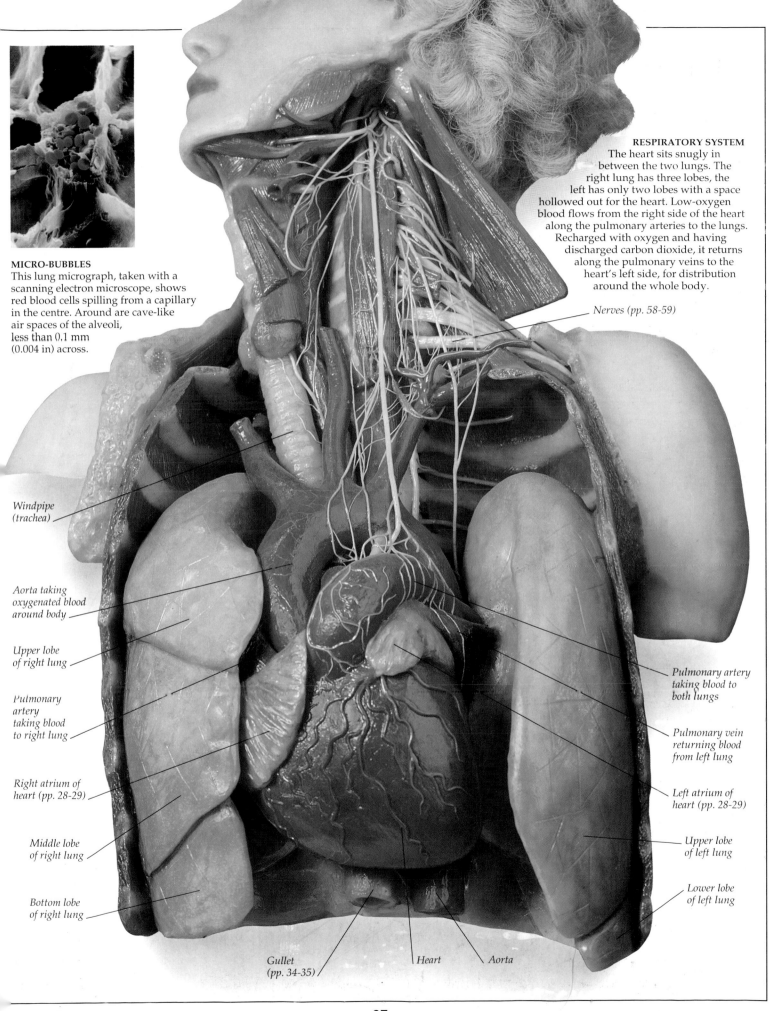

MICRO-BUBBLES
This lung micrograph, taken with a
scanning electron microscope, shows
red blood cells spilling from a capillary
in the centre. Around are cave-like
air spaces of the alveoli,
less than 0.1 mm
(0.004 in) across.

RESPIRATORY SYSTEM
The heart sits snugly in
between the two lungs. The
right lung has three lobes, the
left has only two lobes with a space
hollowed out for the heart. Low-oxygen
blood flows from the right side of the heart
along the pulmonary arteries to the lungs.
Recharged with oxygen and having
discharged carbon dioxide, it returns
along the pulmonary veins to the
heart's left side, for distribution
around the whole body.

Nerves (pp. 58-59)

*Windpipe
(trachea)*

*Aorta taking
oxygenated blood
around body*

*Upper lobe
of right lung*

*Pulmonary
artery
taking blood
to right lung*

*Right atrium of
heart (pp. 28-29)*

*Middle lobe
of right lung*

*Bottom lobe
of right lung*

*Pulmonary artery
taking blood to
both lungs*

*Pulmonary vein
returning blood
from left lung*

*Left atrium of
heart (pp. 28-29)*

*Upper lobe
of left lung*

*Lower lobe
of left lung*

*Gullet
(pp. 34-35)*

Heart

Aorta

The heart

THE HEART IS A STRAIGHTFORWARD, extraordinarily reliable, muscular pump. Its anatomy is relatively simple, yet few body parts have caused so much confusion in their description. In the 4th century BC Aristotle wrote that the heart had three chambers. This is true in creatures such as frogs and lizards, which he had probably examined. However, the human heart, like that of any mammal, has four chambers. There are two on each side: an upper, thin-walled atrium, and a much larger, thick-walled ventricle below. Aristotle also stated that the heart was the seat of intelligence, and this notion persisted in various forms for centuries. Our language today has many references to the heart as the centre of desire, jealousy, loyalty, love, courage, and other emotions, although the brain is the true site. Galen and many after him said that the heart's central dividing wall, the muscular septum, had tiny holes or pores. These allowed blood to seep from one side of the heart to the other. Andreas Vesalius tried to find them by poking hairy bristles at the septum, but he failed – because there are no such pores. Only with William Harvey's work (p. 30) did the real role of the heart as a pump become clear.

THE RIGHT CONNECTIONS
Italian anatomist and botanist Andrea Cesalpino (1519-1603) produced a remarkably accurate description of how the heart was plumbed into the main blood vessels, and connected to the lungs – more than 20 years before Harvey's explanation in *De Motu Cordis*. However, in Cesalpino's last book, he incorrectly stated that the blood flowed out of the heart along all vessels, the veins as well as the arteries.

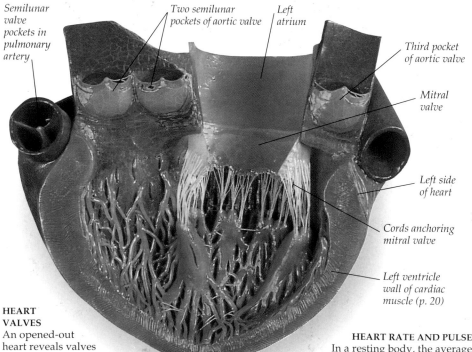

Semilunar valve pockets in pulmonary artery

Two semilunar pockets of aortic valve

Left atrium

Third pocket of aortic valve

Mitral valve

Left side of heart

Cords anchoring mitral valve

Left ventricle wall of cardiac muscle (p. 20)

HEART VALVES
An opened-out heart reveals valves of two types. Between each atrium above ("entrance chamber") and its ventricle below is a large valve, anchored by cords. This is the mitral valve on the body's left side, and on the right the tricuspid valve. The valves prevent a backflow of blood from ventricle to atrium. The cords stop the valves flipping inside out, like an umbrella in high wind. As the ventricles squeeze, blood flows into the arteries (p. 31) through semilunar valves.

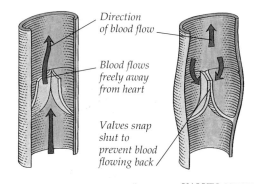

Direction of blood flow

Blood flows freely away from heart

Valves snap shut to prevent blood flowing back

VALVES AT WORK
The semilunar valves at the two exits from the heart have pocket-shaped flaps of tissue fixed strongly into the arterial wall. Blood can push its way out, flattening the flexible pockets against the wall. When the heart pauses before its next beat, the highly pressurized blood in the artery tries to flow back. This opens out the pockets, which balloon together to make a bloodproof seal.

HEART RATE AND PULSE
In a resting body, the average adult heart beats about 60-80 times, pumping around 6 litres (1.3 gal) of blood every minute. Each beat creates a pressure surge through the artery network. The surge can be felt in the radial artery in the wrist, and is called the pulse. During activity, the muscles demand more oxygen and nutrients. The heart beats faster and harder, as much as 150 times a minute, to circulate up to 40 litres (8.8 gal) of blood.

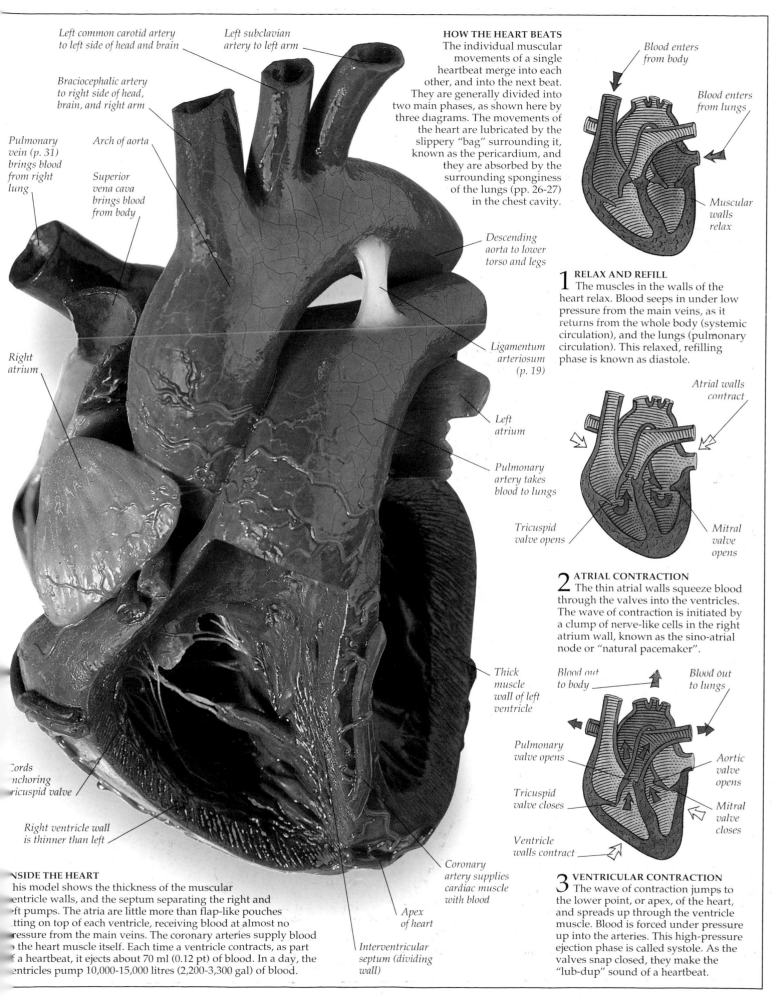

Left common carotid artery to left side of head and brain

Left subclavian artery to left arm

Braciocephalic artery to right side of head, brain, and right arm

Pulmonary vein (p. 31) brings blood from right lung

Arch of aorta

Superior vena cava brings blood from body

Right atrium

Descending aorta to lower torso and legs

Ligamentum arteriosum (p. 19)

Left atrium

Pulmonary artery takes blood to lungs

Thick muscle wall of left ventricle

Cords anchoring tricuspid valve

Right ventricle wall is thinner than left

Coronary artery supplies cardiac muscle with blood

Apex of heart

Interventricular septum (dividing wall)

INSIDE THE HEART
This model shows the thickness of the muscular ventricle walls, and the septum separating the right and left pumps. The atria are little more than flap-like pouches sitting on top of each ventricle, receiving blood at almost no pressure from the main veins. The coronary arteries supply blood to the heart muscle itself. Each time a ventricle contracts, as part of a heartbeat, it ejects about 70 ml (0.12 pt) of blood. In a day, the ventricles pump 10,000-15,000 litres (2,200-3,300 gal) of blood.

HOW THE HEART BEATS
The individual muscular movements of a single heartbeat merge into each other, and into the next beat. They are generally divided into two main phases, as shown here by three diagrams. The movements of the heart are lubricated by the slippery "bag" surrounding it, known as the pericardium, and they are absorbed by the surrounding sponginess of the lungs (pp. 26-27) in the chest cavity.

Blood enters from body

Blood enters from lungs

Muscular walls relax

1 RELAX AND REFILL
The muscles in the walls of the heart relax. Blood seeps in under low pressure from the main veins, as it returns from the whole body (systemic circulation), and the lungs (pulmonary circulation). This relaxed, refilling phase is known as diastole.

Atrial walls contract

Tricuspid valve opens

Mitral valve opens

2 ATRIAL CONTRACTION
The thin atrial walls squeeze blood through the valves into the ventricles. The wave of contraction is initiated by a clump of nerve-like cells in the right atrium wall, known as the sino-atrial node or "natural pacemaker".

Blood out to body

Blood out to lungs

Pulmonary valve opens

Tricuspid valve closes

Aortic valve opens

Mitral valve closes

Ventricle walls contract

3 VENTRICULAR CONTRACTION
The wave of contraction jumps to the lower point, or apex, of the heart, and spreads up through the ventricle muscle. Blood is forced under pressure up into the arteries. This high-pressure ejection phase is called systole. As the valves snap closed, they make the "lub-dup" sound of a heartbeat.

Blood circulation

THE MUSCULAR HEART PUMPS BLOOD out through tubes, or vessels, called arteries. These branch repeatedly into microscopic capillaries, that rejoin to form veins, which carry the blood back to the heart. This idea seems so obvious today that it is difficult to imagine any other way. Even before Aristotle (p. 6) and Galen (p. 9) produced their theories, people invented all sorts of fanciful schemes to explain what the heart and vessels did. A Chinese account in the *Nei Ching* from almost 2,300 years ago, said: "The heart regulates all the blood… the current flows continuously in a circle and never stops". This was probably inspired guesswork, since the book had no anatomical evidence to prove it. After death, arteries collapse and seem to be empty, misleading many scientists. During Ancient Greek times, the arteries were thought to contain air and be part of the windpipe system. Coupled with the ancient beliefs in the four humours (p. 36), confusion reigned in explaining the functions of the heart, vessels, and blood. Some ideas had elements of truth. William Harvey's scheme, published in 1628, at last put science and medicine on the right track.

AIR TO ARTERY
In this 13th-century illustration "life spirit" from inhaled air came into a dark lump in the centre of the heart, where the arteries originated.

ROUND AND ROUND
The credit for establishing the circulatory system is usually given to English physician William Harvey (1578-1657), although Leonardo da Vinci came very close. After experiment and observation, in 1628 Harvey published *De Motu Cordis et Sanguinis in Animalibus*, or "On the Movement of the Heart and Blood in Animals". It stated that blood did not "ebb and flow" in the vessels, as was widely accepted. It circulated round and round, pushed by the heart.

VEIN VALVES
Harvey based his ideas on careful study, rather than blindly following tradition. The approach of his work and his books were the beginning of the era of modern, scientific medicine. His illustrations show how blood in veins always flows towards the heart, as valves prevent it seeping in the wrong direction.

THE BLOOD VESSELS OF THE LEG
The branching nature of the circulatory system is clearly visible in the vessels in the leg. The external iliac artery brings high-oxygen blood into the limb. It divides into branches which in turn subdivide, and subdivide again, progressively becoming smaller. As microscopic capillaries they deliver oxygen and nutrients to the tissues, and collect waste products for removal. They rejoin, forming larger vessels to collect the blood, which join together, and connect into the major veins. The external iliac vein is the main tube draining blood back to the heart.

Small saphenous vein

Posterior tibial vein

Small tibial perforating veins

Figura 1. *Figura 2.*

Calcaneum bone (p. 14)

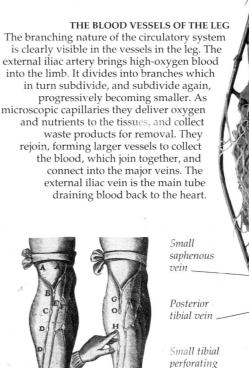

External iliac vein

External iliac artery

Pelvis (pp. 14-15)

Femoral vein

Branch of femoral artery

Great saphenous vein

Knee joint (pp. 16-17)

SELF-BEATING HEART
Swiss-born Albrecht von Haller (1708-1777) was a poet, novelist, and botanist as well as anatomist, and he wrote an eight-volume study of physiology. He investigated how the arteries' muscular walls changed the size of the vessels, so that the amount of blood flowing to different parts of the body could be varied.

Venous arch

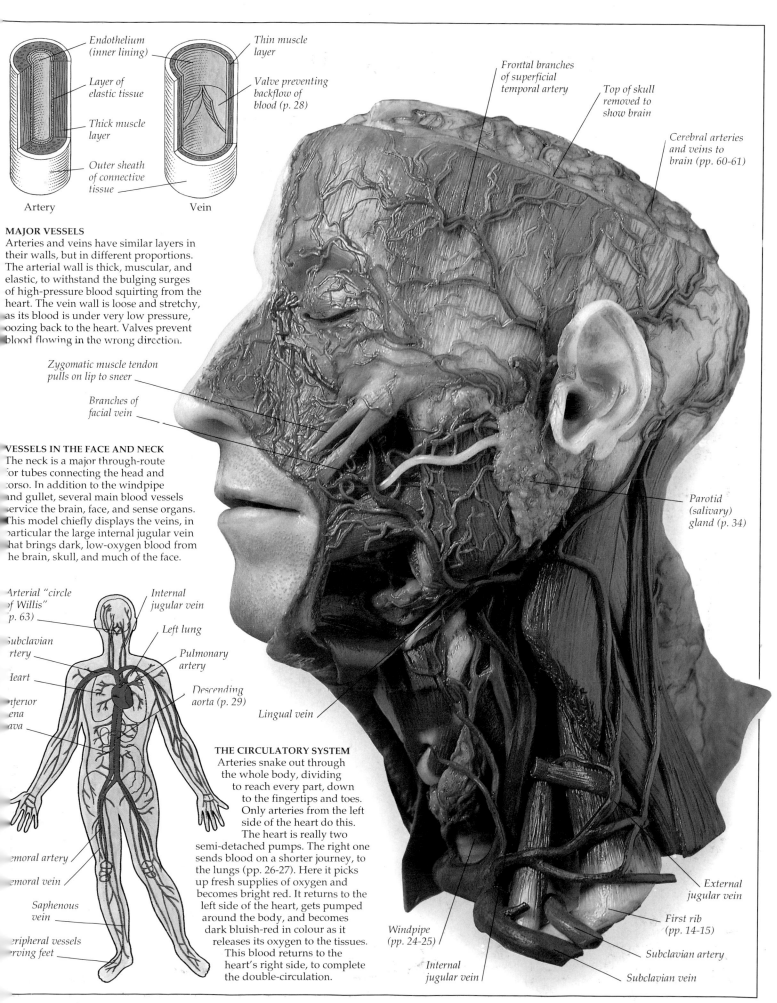

Endothelium (inner lining)

Layer of elastic tissue

Thick muscle layer

Outer sheath of connective tissue

Artery

Thin muscle layer

Valve preventing backflow of blood (p. 28)

Vein

MAJOR VESSELS

Arteries and veins have similar layers in their walls, but in different proportions. The arterial wall is thick, muscular, and elastic, to withstand the bulging surges of high-pressure blood squirting from the heart. The vein wall is loose and stretchy, as its blood is under very low pressure, oozing back to the heart. Valves prevent blood flowing in the wrong direction.

Zygomatic muscle tendon pulls on lip to sneer

Branches of facial vein

VESSELS IN THE FACE AND NECK

The neck is a major through-route for tubes connecting the head and torso. In addition to the windpipe and gullet, several main blood vessels service the brain, face, and sense organs. This model chiefly displays the veins, in particular the large internal jugular vein that brings dark, low-oxygen blood from the brain, skull, and much of the face.

Arterial "circle of Willis" (p. 63)

Subclavian artery

Heart

Inferior vena cava

Femoral artery

Femoral vein

Saphenous vein

Peripheral vessels serving feet

Internal jugular vein

Left lung

Pulmonary artery

Descending aorta (p. 29)

Lingual vein

Frontal branches of superficial temporal artery

Top of skull removed to show brain

Cerebral arteries and veins to brain (pp. 60-61)

Parotid (salivary) gland (p. 34)

External jugular vein

First rib (pp. 14-15)

Subclavian artery

Subclavian vein

Windpipe (pp. 24-25)

Internal jugular vein

THE CIRCULATORY SYSTEM

Arteries snake out through the whole body, dividing to reach every part, down to the fingertips and toes. Only arteries from the left side of the heart do this. The heart is really two semi-detached pumps. The right one sends blood on a shorter journey, to the lungs (pp. 26-27). Here it picks up fresh supplies of oxygen and becomes bright red. It returns to the left side of the heart, gets pumped around the body, and becomes dark bluish-red in colour as it releases its oxygen to the tissues. This blood returns to the heart's right side, to complete the double-circulation.

The blood

A PINHEAD-SIZED DROP OF BLOOD teems with as many as 6 million cells per cubic millimetre. No one saw them until the arrival of the microscope. Before that time, blood was believed to be deeply mysterious, and it was often worshipped and regarded as sacred. It was known to be the very essence of life – as it ebbed away, so the body died. However, little was known of its contents. Physicians of ancient times tasted blood and found it sweet, and guessed it contained sugars. They saw it spurt bright red from cuts in arteries, and realized that it was under pressure. They watched it ooze dark reddish-blue from cuts in veins, and wondered at the colour change. Until the last century blood-letting was popular among doctors who were otherwise stuck for a treatment. It was not until about 1658 that Dutch researcher Jan Swammerdam gazed into his microscope and was the first person to identify and record individual blood cells. Thereafter the microscope became a window into the blood's miniature world of red cells and white cells, platelets, and the liquid portion, plasma.

FEEDING ON BLEEDING
Mosquitoes, fleas, and lice have been sucking blood for millions of years. It is a complete food for them, but blood turns up in superstition, legends, and occult around the world. Many people have believed that by consuming blood, human or animal, qualities such as strength, wisdom, and soul would be passed on. In Bram Stoker's enduring tale of *Dracula* (1897), the Count sucks the blood of young women.

BLOOD TRANSFUSIONS
Since antiquity, people have explored the notion that blood can be transfused (transferred) from one person to another, or even between animals and people, like this 17th-century transfusion from a dog. Some attempts were serious research, others were aimed at dramatic life-saving. More often than not, the blood brought death instead of survival, as the red cells stuck together, or burst open.

BLOOD GROUPS
The reason why red cells may rupture or stick together in a transfusion was unravelled by Austrian scientist Karl Landsteiner (1868-1943) and his colleagues. In certain cases, chemicals in the plasma of one person's blood react with chemicals on the surfaces of the red cells (p. 13) in the other person's blood. The work led to the discovery of the ABO blood group system in the early 1900s, then the M, N, and P systems in 1927. In 1940 the rhesus system was first detected in rhesus monkeys. Today each person's blood is tested, and the transfused blood is selected and matched for maximum safety of the recipient. Landsteiner received the Nobel Prize for Physiology or Medicine in 1930.

Lungs transfer oxygen and carbon dioxide to and from blood (pp. 26-27)

Heart pumps blood around the body (pp. 28-29)

Spleen removes old, worn-out red cells, and helps to recycle their iron (p. 41)

Liver regulates the concentration of many blood chemicals (pp. 36-37)

Stomach and intestines transfer digested nutrients into blood (pp. 36-37)

THE ROLES OF BLOOD
Blood is chiefly used for transport. It fetches and carries in endless journeys around the body. Exchanges between blood and tissues only take place in capillaries, whose walls are so thin that substances can pass through them. Blood spreads another body commodity: heat. It takes warmth from busy organs and muscles to cooler parts, maintaining an even body temperature, and warming the skin and extremities.

WHY IS BLOOD RED?

Dutch microscopist Antoni van Leeuwenhoek proposed that blood's redness is due to the "small globules" we now call red cells, though he would have seen them as pale yellow blobs through his magnifying lens. Each red cell contains a protein called haemoglobin, which is an oxygen transporter. Haemoglobin happens to be bright red when combined with oxygen, and a darker blueish-red when the oxygen has been given up.

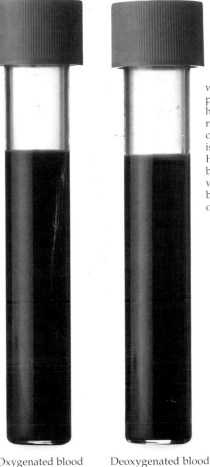

Oxygenated blood   Deoxygenated blood

WHAT IS IN BLOOD?

Allow a blood sample to settle, and it reveals its main components. Just over half (55 per cent) is a pale fluid, plasma. This is more than nine-tenths water and contains dissolved sugars, salts, wastes, body proteins, hormones (p. 40), and many other chemicals. The thin layer, called the buffy coat, is disease-fighting white cells and blood-clotting platelets. The rest, about 45 per cent, is made up of red cells.

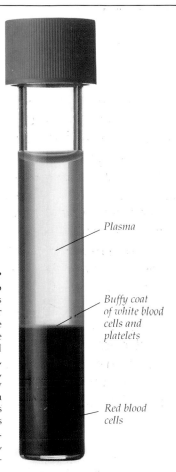

Plasma

Buffy coat of white blood cells and platelets

Red blood cells

Settled blood

RED BLOOD CELLS

Also known as erythrocytes or red corpuscles, red blood cells are some of the smallest cells in the body, 0.007 mm (0.0003 in) across. They are concave on each side. Red cells are made in the bone marrow (p. 17), where they lose their nuclei (control centres), then live for three to four months in the blood.

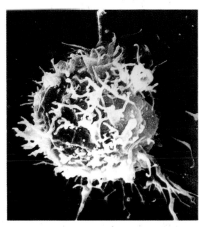

WHITE BLOOD CELLS

Also known as leucocytes or white corpuscles, white blood cells are not really white, but ghostly pale, jelly-like, and able to ooze and change shape. There are several types and sizes. Their main role is to clean the blood, consume debris, and battle against invading viruses and other microbes. To search out invaders they can squeeze between the cells forming the capillary walls, and wander into the surrounding tissues with flowing movements.

STRUCTURE OF HAEMOGLOBIN

Haemoglobin, shown here as a computer-generated molecular model, is a protein made from four intertwined chains of amino acid building blocks, with about 10,000 atoms in total. Four of these are iron atoms (yellow), cradled in four haem rings (green) of amino acids, which act like "oxygen magnets". In the high-oxygen environment of the lungs, each haem group picks up a linked pair of oxygen atoms. In the lower-oxygen tissues, the oxygen atoms detach and drift away, for cellular respiration (p. 24). There are around 300 million molecules of haemoglobin in each red cell.

FORMING BLOOD CLOTS

In a pinprick of blood there are about 5 million red cells, about 10,000 white cells, and a quarter of a million platelets, which are also known as thrombocytes. The platelets are cell fragments from the bone marrow. Damage to a blood vessel begins a cascade of chemical reactions in which a dissolved blood protein, fibrinogen, changes into insoluble threads of fibrin. These form a criss-cross network. Platelets stick to the vessel's walls and the fibrin mesh. Red cells get entangled too, and the whole barrier becomes a clot that seals the leak.

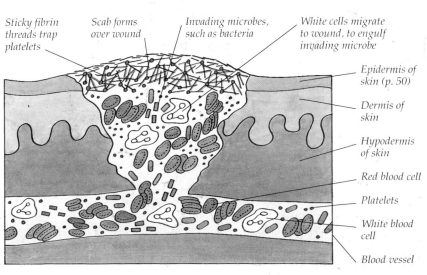

Sticky fibrin threads trap platelets

Scab forms over wound

Invading microbes, such as bacteria

White cells migrate to wound, to engulf invading microbe

Epidermis of skin (p. 50)

Dermis of skin

Hypodermis of skin

Red blood cell

Platelets

White blood cell

Blood vessel

Eating and digestion

FOOD CONTAINS THE body's energy sources and the building blocks for maintenance and repair, as well as being enjoyable and, for some, even a hobby. When you swallow, food travels along the digestive tract, from the mouth, down the gullet (oesophagus) to the stomach, and then on to the small and large intestines. As this tract is relatively large, it has been possible to study the mechanics of digestion since ancient times. Detailed knowledge about the chemistry of digestion, and why the body needs certain types of foods to maintain good health, is relatively recent. Even more recent is a drastic change, particularly in the West, from the age-old and varied human diet of fruits, vegetables, nuts, and some meats, to fast foods, and modern processed foods that are rich in sugar, fat, and salt. So while the digestive system remains stuck in the Stone Age, it is fed by the Space Age. Current nutritional advice now encourages people to try to return to a more natural, better balanced diet.

A BALANCED DIET
There are six main nutrients in food needed for good health: carbohydrates (starches and sugars), fats, proteins, fibres, vitamins, and minerals. A traditional feast in many parts of the world has a different balance of food types to a modern Western meal. There is a good range of starchy foods like rice or potatoes, for energy, and fish for protein. Lots of fresh vegetables and fruits provide fibre, vitamins, and minerals. Few meat and dairy products are needed to provide sufficient protein and fats.

LIFE IN THE "BALLANCE"
Santorio Sanctorius (1561-1636) was a medical professor at Padua in Italy, who had a great enthusiasm for measuring and recording information. For 30 years he spent as much time as he could in his home-made weighing device, the "Ballance". Sanctorius ate, slept, defecated, excreted (pp. 38-39), and he even had sexual intercourse there, carefully measuring his weight changes after each activity. He thought unexplained weight losses might be caused by "invisible vapours" leaving the body.

Teeth (p. 48) are covered with enamel, the body's hardest substance

Tongue

Submandibular salivary gland

CHEWING A MOUTHFUL
Food in the mouth is mixed with a watery substance called saliva, or spit. About 1.5 litres (2.6 p is made daily, in the salivary glands in the sides of the face. At the smell and sight of food, saliva flows along tubes called salivary ducts, into the mouth. Each mouthful of food is lubricated for easier chewing and swallowing. The muscular lips may be sealed to preven dribbles, and the tongue pushes food around for thorough mastication.

The gullet is just behind the windpipe

Windpipe

Gullet *Muscular wave*

CLAUDE BERNARD
French scientist Claude Bernard (1813-1878) is sometimes known as the founder of experimental physiology – investigating the chemical workings of the body. He found that only some stages of digestion take place in the stomach; the rest happen in the small intestine. He also investigated the roles of the liver and pancreas, and pioneered the principle of homeostasis, the idea that constant conditions are maintained inside the body.

X-RAYED SWALLOW
When a mouthful of chewed food is soft and pliable, the tongue squeezes off a portion. The food ball is pushed back and down into the throat, to the top of the gullet. Muscular waves in the gullet's wall propel the lump downwards. In these X-rays the top half of the gullet is shown on the left, and the bottom half on the right. The food contains barium, which shows up white.

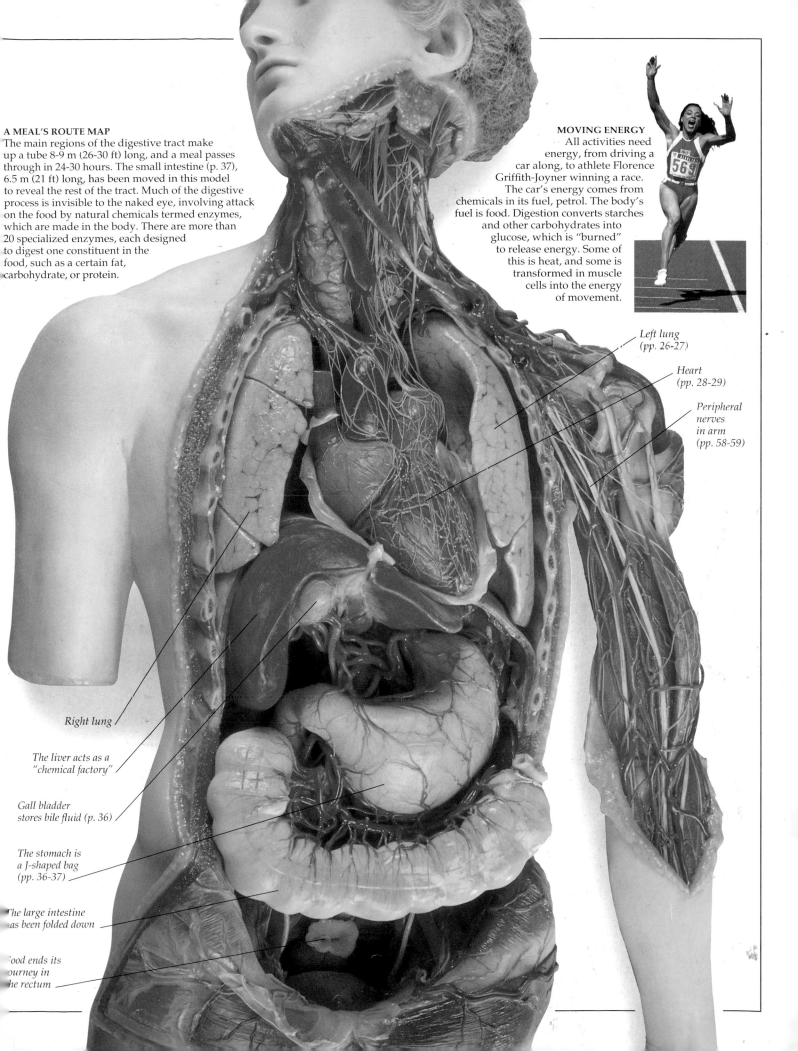

A MEAL'S ROUTE MAP
The main regions of the digestive tract make up a tube 8-9 m (26-30 ft) long, and a meal passes through in 24-30 hours. The small intestine (p. 37), 6.5 m (21 ft) long, has been moved in this model to reveal the rest of the tract. Much of the digestive process is invisible to the naked eye, involving attack on the food by natural chemicals termed enzymes, which are made in the body. There are more than 20 specialized enzymes, each designed to digest one constituent in the food, such as a certain fat, carbohydrate, or protein.

MOVING ENERGY
All activities need energy, from driving a car along, to athlete Florence Griffith-Joyner winning a race. The car's energy comes from chemicals in its fuel, petrol. The body's fuel is food. Digestion converts starches and other carbohydrates into glucose, which is "burned" to release energy. Some of this is heat, and some is transformed in muscle cells into the energy of movement.

Left lung
(pp. 26-27)

Heart
(pp. 28-29)

Peripheral
nerves
in arm
(pp. 58-59)

Right lung

The liver acts as a
"chemical factory"

Gall bladder
stores bile fluid (p. 36)

The stomach is
a J-shaped bag
(pp. 36-37)

The large intestine
has been folded down

Food ends its
journey in
the rectum

Stomach, liver, and intestines

AFTER FOOD IS SWALLOWED IT TRAVELS in soft lumps down the gullet into the stomach. This stretches as it fills, to hold 2 litres (3.5 pt) or more. The stomach is both food mixer and acid-and-enzyme bath. Every few minutes its strong, muscular walls undergo a spasm of squeezing to churn the food into a semiliquid called chyme. Only a few substances are actually absorbed through the stomach lining into the blood. The next stage of the digestive tube is the small intestine, where chemical digestion continues and most nutrients are absorbed. Inside a healthy intestine live "friendly" bacteria. They can make important nutrients such as vitamin K, help to break down thick cellulose walls of plant cells, and are involved in processing bile salts. Both members of this partnership benefit – the bacteria have a warm, food-rich place to live, and the body obtains nutrients it would otherwise miss. The large intestine forms the leftovers into brownish, semisolid masses, ready for disposal.

ANCIENT HUMOURS
In ancient times a popular theory, adopted by physicians for centuries afterwards, involved four fluids, or humours, contained by the body: blood, mucus (phlegm), black bile, and yellow bile. The balance of the humours determined a person's temperament. Blood, or *Sanguis*, made a person sanguine; phlegm, or *Pituita*, was phlegmatic; yellow bile, or *Chole*, was choleric; black bile, or *Melanchole*, was melancholic. Humoral imbalance was believed to be the cause of illness.

FOOD-PROCESSING STOMACH
The stomach has three layers of muscle fibres, which run lengthways, crossways, and diagonally. Between them they can contort the stomach into almost any shape. The stomach digests up to half of the carbohydrates in a meal, one tenth of the protein, but hardly any fat. Up to six hours after eating, soupy chyme is still being squirted into the small intestine.

Gullet (oesophagus)

Top layer of muscle fibres running lengthways

Main body of stomach

THE LIVER'S CHEMICAL "FACTORY"
The body's largest internal organ is the liver. Soft, and a rich dark-red with blood, it has a large right lobe and a much smaller left lobe. Blood flows to the liver directly from the heart, and also from the intestines. The blood oozes through some 50,000 tiny units called hepatic lobules, about 1 mm (0.04 in) across. Here chemical processes break down digested nutrients even further, assemble useful substances, filter old cells from blood, and store or release sugars, starches, fats, vitamins, and minerals, according to the body's changing needs.

Pancreas

Duodenum

Pancreas

Gall bladder

PANCREATIC ENZYMES
The wedge-shaped pancreas has two distinct roles. As an endocrine gland it makes the hormone insulin (p. 41). As an exocrine (ducted) gland it produces pancreatic juices packed with enzymes that digest carbohydrates, proteins, and particularly fats. Each day 1.5 litres (2.6 pt) of these juices flow along the pancreatic duct, and into the duodenum of the small intestine.

FATS, BILE, AND THE GALL BLADDER
The soft, elastic gall bladder is a stretchy bag that stores greenish-brown bile fluid. Bile contains wastes from the liver, and broken-down blood cells which give its colour. It passes along the bile duct into the duodenum, where its salts break up fats into tiny droplets for better absorption.

Liver   *Bile duct*

Inferior vena cava (vein)

Exit of bile duct into duodenum

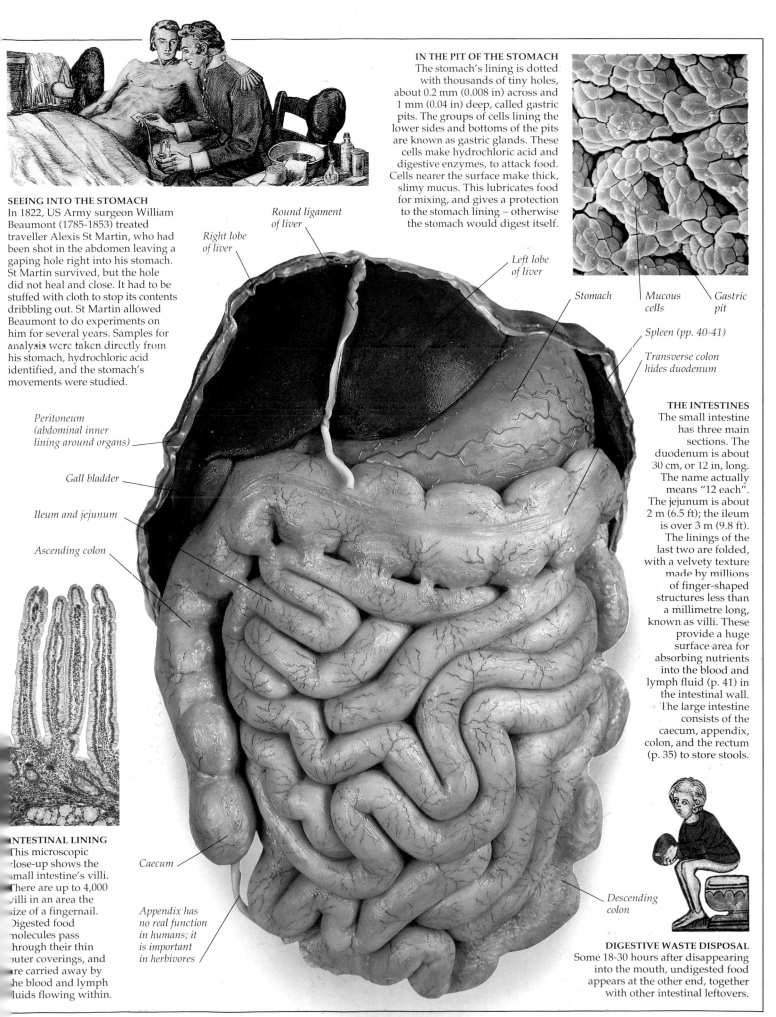

SEEING INTO THE STOMACH

In 1822, US Army surgeon William Beaumont (1785-1853) treated traveller Alexis St Martin, who had been shot in the abdomen leaving a gaping hole right into his stomach. St Martin survived, but the hole did not heal and close. It had to be stuffed with cloth to stop its contents dribbling out. St Martin allowed Beaumont to do experiments on him for several years. Samples for analysis were taken directly from his stomach, hydrochloric acid identified, and the stomach's movements were studied.

IN THE PIT OF THE STOMACH

The stomach's lining is dotted with thousands of tiny holes, about 0.2 mm (0.008 in) across and 1 mm (0.04 in) deep, called gastric pits. The groups of cells lining the lower sides and bottoms of the pits are known as gastric glands. These cells make hydrochloric acid and digestive enzymes, to attack food. Cells nearer the surface make thick, slimy mucus. This lubricates food for mixing, and gives a protection to the stomach lining – otherwise the stomach would digest itself.

Round ligament of liver

Right lobe of liver

Left lobe of liver

Stomach

Mucous cells

Gastric pit

Spleen (pp. 40-41)

Transverse colon hides duodenum

Peritoneum (abdominal inner lining around organs)

Gall bladder

Ileum and jejunum

Ascending colon

THE INTESTINES

The small intestine has three main sections. The duodenum is about 30 cm, or 12 in, long. The name actually means "12 each". The jejunum is about 2 m (6.5 ft); the ileum is over 3 m (9.8 ft). The linings of the last two are folded, with a velvety texture made by millions of finger-shaped structures less than a millimetre long, known as villi. These provide a huge surface area for absorbing nutrients into the blood and lymph fluid (p. 41) in the intestinal wall. The large intestine consists of the caecum, appendix, colon, and the rectum (p. 35) to store stools.

INTESTINAL LINING

This microscopic close-up shows the small intestine's villi. There are up to 4,000 villi in an area the size of a fingernail. Digested food molecules pass through their thin outer coverings, and are carried away by the blood and lymph fluids flowing within.

Caecum

Appendix has no real function in humans; it is important in herbivores

Descending colon

DIGESTIVE WASTE DISPOSAL

Some 18-30 hours after disappearing into the mouth, undigested food appears at the other end, together with other intestinal leftovers.

Getting rid of wastes

LIKE ANY COMPLEX MACHINE, the human body produces several waste products. Lungs breathe out carbon dioxide gas; the digestive tract expels leftover food and other matter as faeces; the skin sweats out certain salts. Another waste is urine. The kidneys filter undesirable substances, with unwanted water, from the blood. Urine is stored in a bag, the bladder, before being expelled. The kidneys and bladder, and their various connecting tubes, are known as the urinary, or excretory, system. One of the earliest accurate descriptions of the system was in Aristotle's *Historia Animalium*. It showed the two kidneys, the ureter pipes that connect them to the bladder, and the urethra, the exit tube from the bladder. Study with the naked eye did not reveal how the kidneys worked, and there was little progress from Aristotle until the age of the microscope, when Marcello Malpighi (p.12) identified the glomerulus in the 1650s. Today we have a detailed understanding of how one million nephrons in each kidney filter blood to make urine.

GIANT OF ANCIENT GREECE
Aristotle (384-322 BC) is also known as the "father of nature and biology". Generations of philosophers continued traditional beliefs while paying little attention to the real world around them. Aristotle moved away from this and he was one of the first people to look inside real bodies, mostly animal, and record what he saw. He was also a pioneer in the grouping of living things according to features they shared. Such classification underlies modern science.

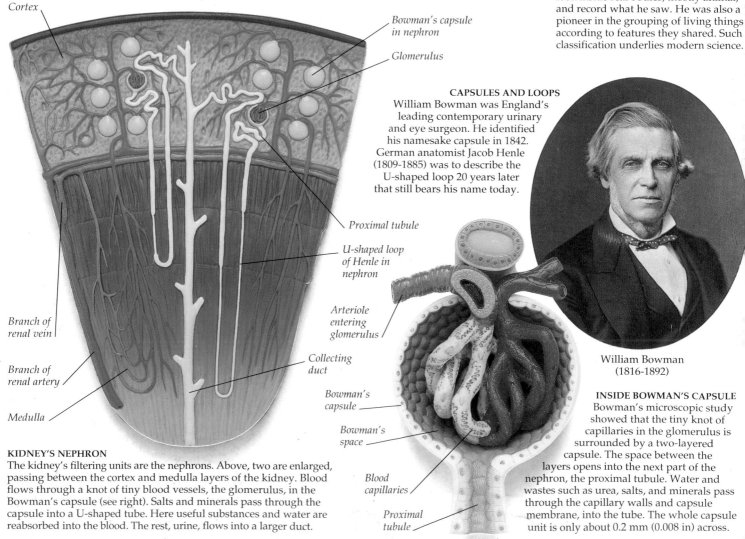

Cortex

Bowman's capsule in nephron

Glomerulus

CAPSULES AND LOOPS
William Bowman was England's leading contemporary urinary and eye surgeon. He identified his namesake capsule in 1842. German anatomist Jacob Henle (1809-1885) was to describe the U-shaped loop 20 years later that still bears his name today.

Proximal tubule

U-shaped loop of Henle in nephron

Arteriole entering glomerulus

Branch of renal vein

Branch of renal artery

Collecting duct

Medulla

Bowman's capsule

William Bowman (1816-1892)

Bowman's space

INSIDE BOWMAN'S CAPSULE
Bowman's microscopic study showed that the tiny knot of capillaries in the glomerulus is surrounded by a two-layered capsule. The space between the layers opens into the next part of the nephron, the proximal tubule. Water and wastes such as urea, salts, and minerals pass through the capillary walls and capsule membrane, into the tube. The whole capsule unit is only about 0.2 mm (0.008 in) across.

KIDNEY'S NEPHRON
The kidney's filtering units are the nephrons. Above, two are enlarged, passing between the cortex and medulla layers of the kidney. Blood flows through a knot of tiny blood vessels, the glomerulus, in the Bowman's capsule (see right). Salts and minerals pass through the capsule into a U-shaped tube. Here useful substances and water are reabsorbed into the blood. The rest, urine, flows into a larger duct.

Blood capillaries

Proximal tubule

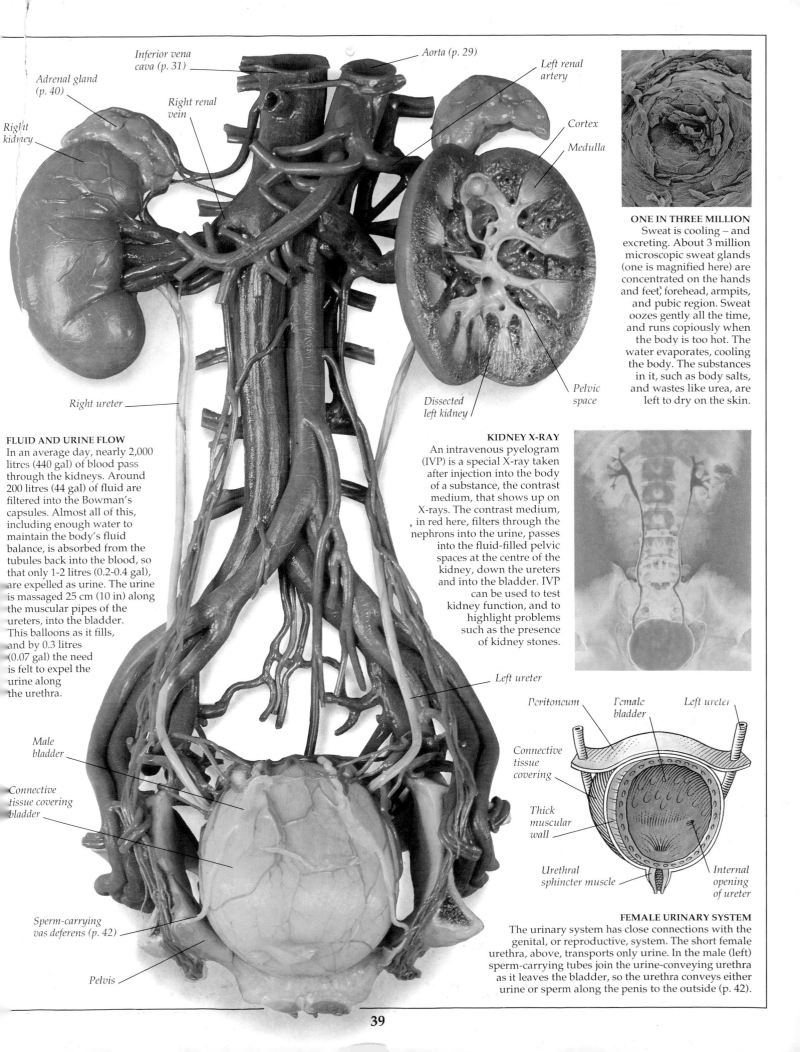

Inferior vena cava (p. 31)

Aorta (p. 29)

Left renal artery

Adrenal gland (p. 40)

Right renal vein

Right kidney

Cortex

Medulla

Right ureter

Dissected left kidney

Pelvic space

ONE IN THREE MILLION
Sweat is cooling – and excreting. About 3 million microscopic sweat glands (one is magnified here) are concentrated on the hands and feet, forehead, armpits, and pubic region. Sweat oozes gently all the time, and runs copiously when the body is too hot. The water evaporates, cooling the body. The substances in it, such as body salts, and wastes like urea, are left to dry on the skin.

FLUID AND URINE FLOW
In an average day, nearly 2,000 litres (440 gal) of blood pass through the kidneys. Around 200 litres (44 gal) of fluid are filtered into the Bowman's capsules. Almost all of this, including enough water to maintain the body's fluid balance, is absorbed from the tubules back into the blood, so that only 1-2 litres (0.2-0.4 gal), are expelled as urine. The urine is massaged 25 cm (10 in) along the muscular pipes of the ureters, into the bladder. This balloons as it fills, and by 0.3 litres (0.07 gal) the need is felt to expel the urine along the urethra.

KIDNEY X-RAY
An intravenous pyelogram (IVP) is a special X-ray taken after injection into the body of a substance, the contrast medium, that shows up on X-rays. The contrast medium, in red here, filters through the nephrons into the urine, passes into the fluid-filled pelvic spaces at the centre of the kidney, down the ureters and into the bladder. IVP can be used to test kidney function, and to highlight problems such as the presence of kidney stones.

Left ureter

Male bladder

Connective tissue covering bladder

Peritoneum

Female bladder

Left ureter

Connective tissue covering

Thick muscular wall

Urethral sphincter muscle

Internal opening of ureter

Sperm-carrying vas deferens (p. 42)

Pelvis

FEMALE URINARY SYSTEM
The urinary system has close connections with the genital, or reproductive, system. The short female urethra, above, transports only urine. In the male (left) sperm-carrying tubes join the urine-conveying urethra as it leaves the bladder, so the urethra conveys either urine or sperm along the penis to the outside (p. 42).

Body chemistry

REDUCE THE BODY TO ITS BASICS, and it is like a complicated chemical factory. Every second, millions of substances take part in chemical reactions. The overall process of body chemistry is called metabolism. Physiologists are people who unravel its intricacies – how the organs and tissues function. Physiology is a complementary subject to anatomy, the study of structure. Muscles, bones, nerves, and guts all have characteristic chemical pathways. Three other chemical-based systems involve the whole body. These are the blood circulation (pp. 30-33), the endocrine or hormonal system, and the lymphatic system. Endocrinology is the study of hormones, the body's chemical messengers. It is a fairly recent science, begun in earnest only about a century ago. Lymph is a circulating fluid known as "blood's distant relative". It has only a vague system of vessels, and no pump of its own in the way that blood has the heart (pp. 28-29), but it is vital to defend the body against disease and infection.

FIGHT OR FLIGHT
The hormone adrenaline prepares the body for physical action in the face of danger. It slows the digestive system (p. 34) and constricts blood vessels (pp. 50-51) to the skin to make more blood available to the muscles. The blood races and the muscles tense. This helps to fight the danger, in this case a bull, or flee from it.

EXCITING GLANDS
The body has more than 50 hormones – messenger chemicals made by endocrine glands. The main endocrine glands are shown on the left. The hormones are released straight into the blood flowing through the glands. They spread around the body, and they excite or stimulate certain parts, known as their target tissues and organs. The word hormone is from the Greek *hormon*, meaning "to stir up" or "excite". It was suggested in 1905 by English physiologist Ernest Starling (1866-1927), three years after he helped to isolate the first hormone, secretin, from the intestine.

THYROID GLAND
Like an internal bow tie in the neck, the thyroid gland makes three main hormones. Thyroxine and triiodothyronine control growth and metabolic rate, and in excess increase pulse rate and intestinal contractions felt as "butterflies in the stomach". Calcitonin channels calcium from the blood, to be stored in the bones.

ADRENAL GLANDS
One adrenal, or "suprarenal", gland sits on top of each kidney – another name for the kidney is the renal gland. The adrenal's outer part, the cortex, makes several hormones called corticosteroids. They include aldosterone to conserve salt and water in the kidneys, glucocorticoid steroids to speed up the metabolism and cope with stress, and the sex hormones (pp. 42-43). The inner part, or medulla, produces adrenaline, which readies the body for action in the fight-or-flight response.

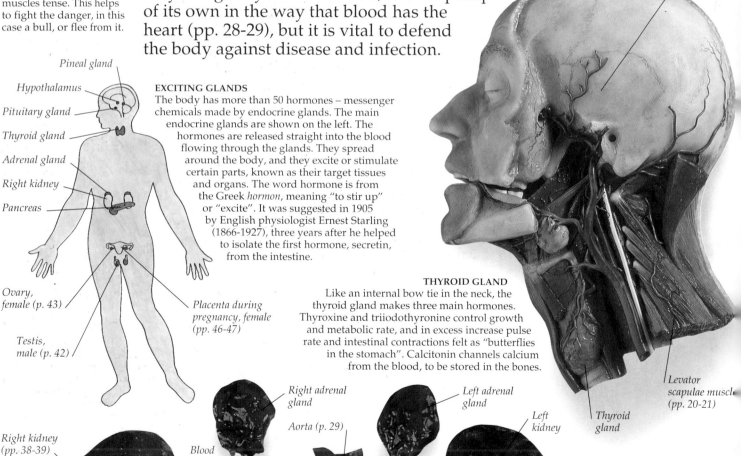

Pineal gland
Hypothalamus
Pituitary gland
Thyroid gland
Adrenal gland
Right kidney
Pancreas
Ovary, female (p. 43)
Testis, male (p. 42)
Placenta during pregnancy, female (pp. 46-47)

Temporal bone (p. 15)

Levator scapulae muscle (pp. 20-21)

Thyroid gland

Right adrenal gland
Aorta (p. 29)
Left adrenal gland
Left kidney
Blood vessels to adrenal gland
Right kidney (pp. 38-39)
Right renal vein (pp. 30-31)

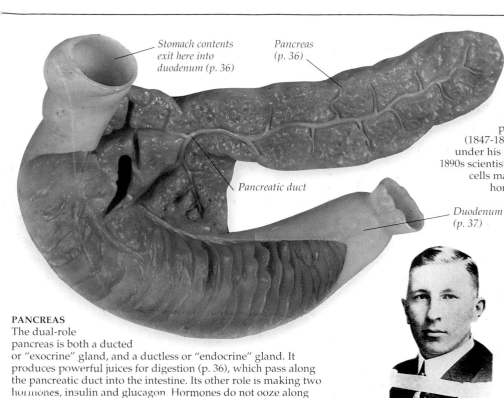

Stomach contents
exit here into
duodenum (p. 36)

Pancreas
(p. 36)

Pancreatic duct

Duodenum
(p. 37)

PANCREATIC ISLETS

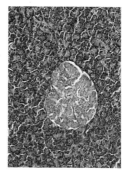

The pancreas (p. 36) is
dotted with more than
1 million tiny clumps
of cells known as islets
of Langerhans; one is
shown, right. They are
named after the German
physician Paul Langerhans
(1847-1888), who discovered them
under his microscope in 1869. In the
1890s scientists discovered that the islet
cells made secretions, later called
hormones, including insulin.

PANCREAS

The dual-role
pancreas is both a ducted
or "exocrine" gland, and a ductless or "endocrine" gland. It
produces powerful juices for digestion (p. 36), which pass along
the pancreatic duct into the intestine. Its other role is making two
hormones, insulin and glucagon. Hormones do not ooze along
ducts. They seep directly into blood (pp. 32-33) flowing through
the organ, past the manufacturing cells. The balance of insulin
and glucagon controls the level of glucose (sugar) in the blood.

THE INSULIN STORY

The hormone insulin tells the
liver to change glucose into
starch and store it. In 1922
Canadian Frederick Banting
and American Charles Best
announced that they had
extracted insulin and tested
it on dogs with diabetes, a
serious condition caused by
lack of insulin. Banting
and laboratory director
J. Macleod received a
Nobel Prize in 1923.

Sir Frederick Banting
(1891-1941)

Charles Best
(1899-1978)

The lymphatic system

Lymph is a milky liquid that begins as watery fluids which
have collected in spaces around cells (pp. 12-13), and
watery fluids which have leaked from small blood vessels
(pp. 30-31). These fluids channel slowly into a body-wide
system of tubes like veins, with one-way valves. Lymph has
several jobs. It collects wastes from cell activity; it distributes
nutrients, especially fats; it also carries white blood cells
(p. 33) around the body in the fight against infection.

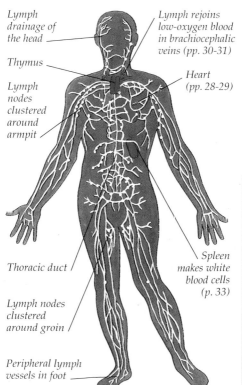

Lymph
drainage of
the head

Lymph rejoins
low-oxygen blood
in brachiocephalic
veins (pp. 30-31)

Thymus

Heart
(pp. 28-29)

Lymph
nodes
clustered
around
armpit

Thoracic duct

Spleen
makes white
blood cells
(p. 33)

Lymph nodes
clustered
around groin

Peripheral lymph
vessels in foot

SLOW CIRCULATOR

The system of lymph vessels is almost as
extensive as the blood system, but it is only
"half" a circulation as it has no pump. A person
has about 1 litre (1.8 pt) of lymph, on average. It
oozes along its vessels, propelled indirectly by
the pressure of the blood, and by the body's
muscles which "massage" the vessel walls. The
major lymph vessels empty their fluid back into
the blood, in the main veins near the heart.

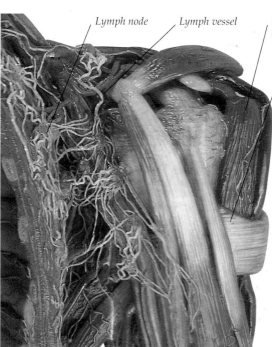

Lymph node

Lymph vessel

Shoulder muscle
(pp. 20-21)

Model of
dissected
arm

THYMUS GLAND

Two main glands are associated with
the lymph system, the spleen (p. 32),
and the thymus in the upper chest.
The thymus is large in childhood, but
shrinks during adult life. It helps to
"train" white blood cells to recognize
germs and other body invaders. The
electron microscope shows the
cortex (outer area) of the thymus.
The spheres are a type of white
blood cell, called lymphocytes.

LYMPH NODES

Lymph vessels widen at intervals to form
lymph nodes, which vary from the size of
grape pips to larger than whole grapes. The
nodes clean and filter the lymph, and store
germ-fighting white blood cells. In several
body regions, nodes are clustered together, as
shown here in the armpit. These nodes are the
so-called "glands" that swell up and become
hard during illness, due to their contents of
millions of white blood cells and dead germs.

Males and females

Reproduction is the hallmark of life – a vital part of the cycle of living things. In the human species, reproduction is much the same as for any other mammal. Specialized reproductive organs are in the lower abdomen. The male has glands called testes that make microscopic, tadpole-shaped sperm cells. The female has glands called ovaries that make pinpoint-sized egg cells. To begin a new life, a sperm cell must fertilize an egg cell, and sexual intercourse brings these cells together. Pioneer scientific anatomists such as Leonardo da Vinci and Andreas Vesalius treated the sexual organs like any other parts of the body, making careful dissections and increasingly accurate depictions. Yet through history, there have been varying and inaccurate views of the reproductive organs and of mating, for example Aristotle denied any female contribution to a "soul". Some societies regard sexual acts as a natural, unremarkable aspect of life. Other cultures surround sex with taboos, keep it furtive, secret, and suppressed, or even worship it.

BEGINNER'S GUIDE
In the 1540s Andreas Vesalius (p. 10) presented the typical male and female human bodies, in his book *Epitome*. The male is generally more muscular than the female, with wide shoulders and narrow hips, and more facial and body hair. The female overall contours are rounded by pads of body fat, particularly around the thighs and abdomen, with wide hips and developed breasts. *Epitome* was intended as a "beginner's" guide to anatomy. The drawings identified the external features of the body.

MALE REPRODUCTIVE ORGANS
The model shows a cutaway view of the male reproductive system. It is closely linked to the urinary system (pp. 38-39), as the urethra inside the penis is a tube for both urine and sperm cells. The two oval testes in their skin bag, the scrotum, make millions of sperms every day. These are stored in 500 m (547 yd) of tiny, tightly-coiled tubes in each testis, and in the 6-m (6.6-yd), spaghetti-like tangle of tubes forming the epididymis. During sex, muscle contractions propel the sperms along the sperm ducts and urethra, and out of the penis.

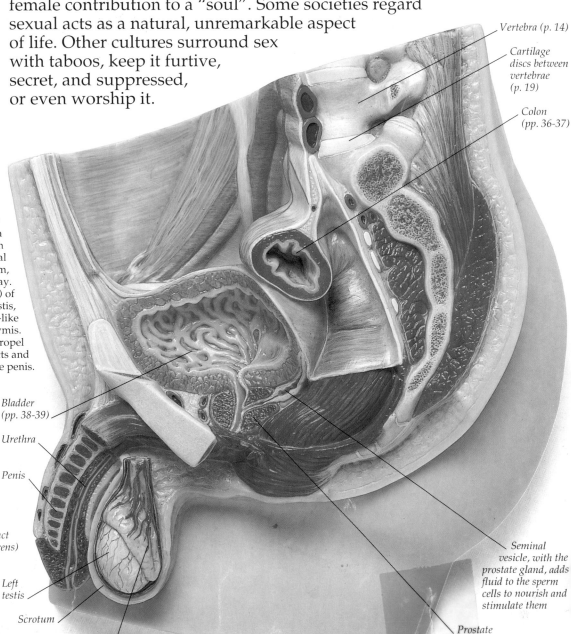

Vertebra (p. 14)

Cartilage discs between vertebrae (p. 19)

Colon (pp. 36-37)

Seminal vesicle, with the prostate gland, adds fluid to the sperm cells to nourish and stimulate them

Prostate gland

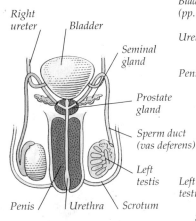

Right ureter *Bladder*

Seminal gland

Prostate gland

Sperm duct (vas deferens)

Left testis

Penis *Urethra* *Scrotum*

Front view of male reproductive system

Bladder (pp. 38-39)

Urethra

Penis

Left testis

Scrotum

Epididymis

The menstrual cycle

A man's testes make sperms all the time. If not released, they die, and are reabsorbed. The female system goes through hormonal changes (pp. 40-41) in a cycle lasting about four weeks, known as the menstrual cycle. The cycle occurs from puberty until the menopause, unless pregnancy begins.

RIPE EGG
Each egg cell ripens in a fluid-filled container called a follicle, like a blister on the ovary's surface. This electron micrograph shows a just-released (ovulated) egg cell (red), ready to enter the oviduct. It has left the ripe Graafian follicle (upper left).

REGNIER DE GRAAF
Dutch anatomist Regnier de Graaf (1641-1673) carried out many important studies at Delft. After work on the analysis of pancreatic juices (p. 36), he published detailed works on the male and female reproductive organs, in 1668 and 1672. He identified the tiny "bubbles" on the ovary's surface as ova, or eggs. Later it was discovered that each bubble is a ripe follicle, or egg-container, with the much smaller egg inside it. About 90 years later von Haller (p. 30) named them Graafian follicles in his honour.

HORMONE CONTROL
Follicle-stimulating hormone from the pituitary gland (p. 57) ripens the egg follicle. Luteinizing hormone from the pituitary stimulates the follicle to release its egg at ovulation. The empty follicle is called a corpus luteum, and makes the hormone progesterone. This, with oestrogen from the ovary, thicken the uterus lining.

Egg   *Oviduct*   *Uterus lining*   *Egg*
Period

1 FIRST WEEK The thickened lining of the uterus, prepared to nourish a fertilized egg, breaks down and is lost as blood flow out of the vagina (the period).

2 SECOND WEEK An egg ripens near the surface of one of the ovaries, to become a Graafian follicle. The uterus lining begins to grow and thicken again.

3 THIRD WEEK The egg bursts from its container or follicle and moves along the oviduct, massaged by muscles and microscopic cilia hairs in its lining.

4 FOURTH WEEK The egg reaches the uterus. It has not joined with a sperm, so the blood-rich uterus lining is not needed, and the cycle starts over again.

FEMALE REPRODUCTIVE ORGANS
In this model, the right ovary is against the abdominal wall, while the uterus is cut in section. When a ripe egg leaves its follicle it is caught by the finger-like fimbriae and wafted into the trumpet-shaped ampulla. This leads to the curving oviduct, also called the fallopian tube after anatomist and nobleman Gabriele Fallopius of Italy (1523-1562). Fallopius published the first detailed account of this tube in 1561. The oviduct opens into the upper corner of the hollow, pear-shaped uterus. If the egg does not meet a sperm cell and become fertilized, it dies and is lost with the menstrual blood during the period.

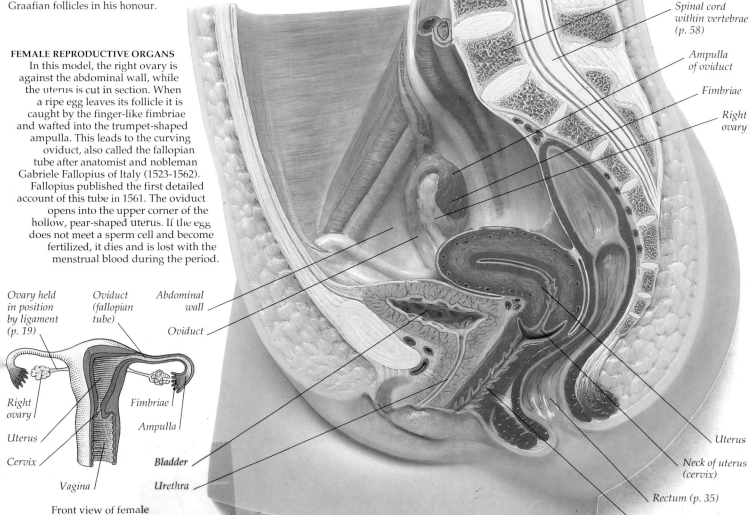

Vertebra

Spinal cord within vertebrae (p. 58)

Ampulla of oviduct

Fimbriae

Right ovary

Uterus

Neck of uterus (cervix)

Rectum (p. 35)

Vagina

Ovary held in position by ligament (p. 19)

Oviduct (fallopian tube)

Abdominal wall

Oviduct

Right ovary

Fimbriae

Uterus

Ampulla

Cervix

Bladder

Vagina

Urethra

Front view of female reproductive system

A new life

THE TIME IN THE WOMB IS THE FIRST, yet largely unseen, part of a baby's life. It is the period between an egg joining with a sperm cell at fertilization, and the resulting baby's entrance into the world, at birth. A female human is pregnant for about 266 days. A female mouse is pregnant for about 20 days, and a female elephant for some 660 days. Our species follows the general trend in the mammal group – the larger the body size, the longer the pregnancy. In fact, almost everything about pregnancy in humans follows the standard mammal pattern. Knowledge of pregnancy has come a long way since Aristotle's views. He stated that the father provided the soul and spirit for the baby. The mother provided the menstrual blood, which mixed with semen fluid from the father, and remained in the womb to give rise to the baby. The mother was thought to be simply a carrier or "incubator", feeding and providing for the life-force that originated from the man.

FIRST EMBRYOLOGIST
In 1604, Italian professor Hieronymus Fabricius (1537-1619) published *De Formato Foetu*, a study about the development of eggs and unborn babies in a range of animals, including humans. Even in his lifetime, Fabricius was known as the founder of embryology. He named the ovary, the egg-making organ in the chicken, and predicted its function.

SEXUAL INTERCOURSE
In the 1950s and 1960s, scientists carried out detailed research into sexual intercourse. The woman's vagina (p. 43) expands and moistens with mucous secretions. The man's penis (p. 42) fills with blood, and becomes erect. In the orgasmic phase of the male, the muscles around the sex organs contract rhythmically, and sperm cells in their semen fluid are ejaculated into the woman's vagina. After orgasm, the muscles and sex organs relax and return to normal, and the partners sometimes feel drowsy.

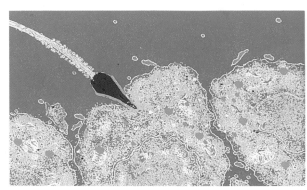

FERTILIZATION OF THE EGG CELL
In this electron micrograph, a sperm cell is penetrating the follicular cells around the egg cell (p. 43). The sperm cell is about one-twentieth of a millimetre long, and most of this is its long tail, trailing off towards the top left in the picture. There are about 300-500 million sperm in the semen fluid, but only one sperm can fertilize the egg.

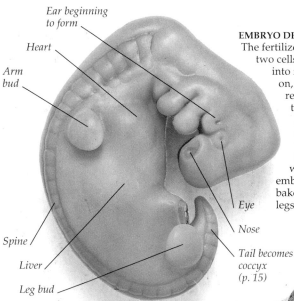

Ear beginning to form

Heart

Arm bud

Spine

Liver

Leg bud

Eye

Nose

Tail becomes coccyx (p. 15)

EMBRYO DEVELOPMENT
The fertilized egg divides into two cells (pp. 48-49), then into four, then eight, and so on, every few hours. The resulting hundreds, and then thousands of cells gradually group together, and change into different types such as muscle, nerve and blood cells. Five weeks after fertilization, the embryo is smaller than a baked bean, yet its arms and legs are already developing.

FETAL DEVELOPMENT
About two months after fertilization, all of the major organs have formed, and the baby's heart is beating, and yet its body is still just 25 mm (1 in) long. Embryologists through the ages have been amazed at the similarity between the early embryos of humans, monkeys, cats, and many other types of mammals. From two months through to birth the developing baby gradually comes to look distinctly human. It is known as a fetus, from the Latin for "offspring".

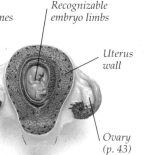

Recognizable embryo limbs

Uterus wall

Ovary (p. 43)

1 TWO MONTHS
The baby is smaller than a walnut, and tiny fingers and toes are growing. The pregnancy is confirmed.

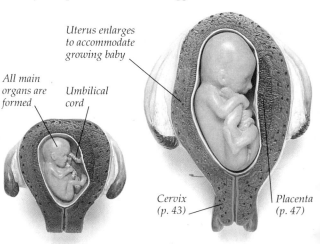

All main organs are formed

Umbilical cord

Uterus enlarges to accommodate growing baby

Cervix (p. 43)

Placenta (p. 47)

2 THREE MONTHS
About 70 mm (2.8 in) long, the baby can move its head and limbs. The mother hardly feels this.

3 FIVE MONTHS
The baby is 25 cm (10 in) long, and responds to loud sounds by kicking and turning somersaults. The mother's abdomen bulges.

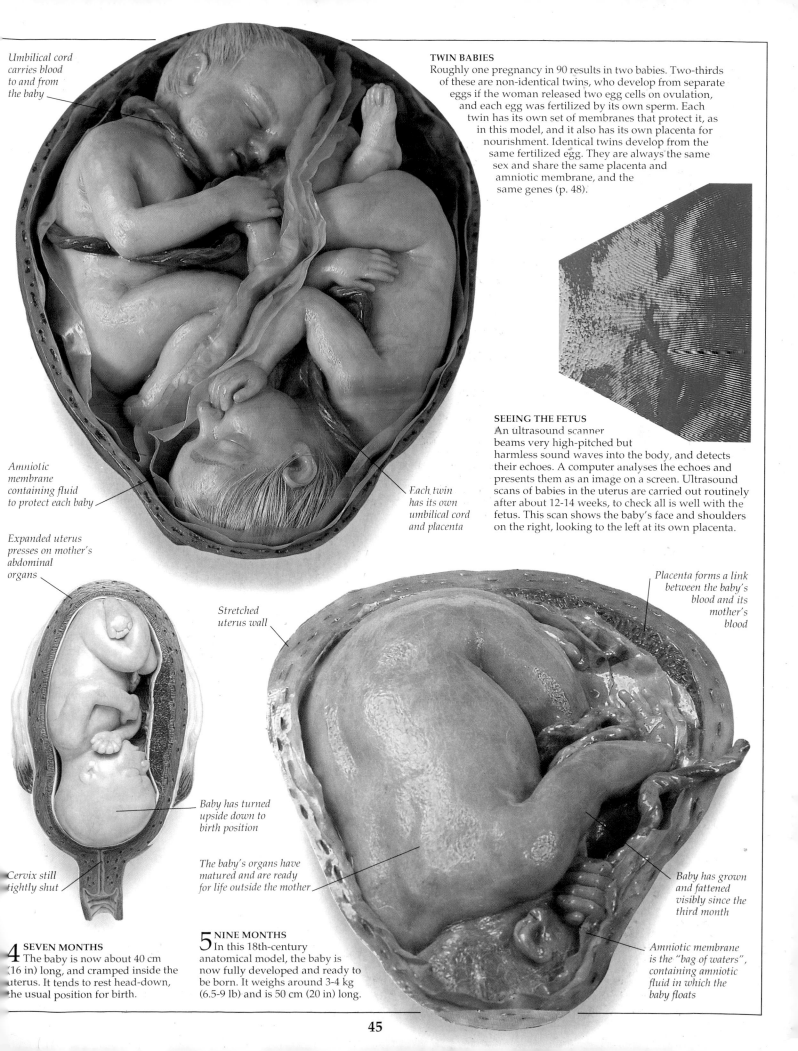

Umbilical cord carries blood to and from the baby

TWIN BABIES
Roughly one pregnancy in 90 results in two babies. Two-thirds of these are non-identical twins, who develop from separate eggs if the woman released two egg cells on ovulation, and each egg was fertilized by its own sperm. Each twin has its own set of membranes that protect it, as in this model, and it also has its own placenta for nourishment. Identical twins develop from the same fertilized egg. They are always the same sex and share the same placenta and amniotic membrane, and the same genes (p. 48).

Amniotic membrane containing fluid to protect each baby

SEEING THE FETUS
An ultrasound scanner beams very high-pitched but harmless sound waves into the body, and detects their echoes. A computer analyses the echoes and presents them as an image on a screen. Ultrasound scans of babies in the uterus are carried out routinely after about 12-14 weeks, to check all is well with the fetus. This scan shows the baby's face and shoulders on the right, looking to the left at its own placenta.

Each twin has its own umbilical cord and placenta

Expanded uterus presses on mother's abdominal organs

Placenta forms a link between the baby's blood and its mother's blood

Stretched uterus wall

Baby has turned upside down to birth position

The baby's organs have matured and are ready for life outside the mother

Baby has grown and fattened visibly since the third month

Cervix still tightly shut

Amniotic membrane is the "bag of waters", containing amniotic fluid in which the baby floats

4 SEVEN MONTHS
The baby is now about 40 cm (16 in) long, and cramped inside the uterus. It tends to rest head-down, the usual position for birth.

5 NINE MONTHS
In this 18th-century anatomical model, the baby is now fully developed and ready to be born. It weighs around 3-4 kg (6.5-9 lb) and is 50 cm (20 in) long.

Birth and baby

IN THEORY, THE PROCESS OF CHILDBIRTH is relatively simple. The neck, or cervix, of the mother's uterus, which is tightly closed during pregnancy, relaxes and widens (dilates). The uterus muscles begin to tense and shorten in waves called contractions, which become more frequent and powerful. This stage is called labour – aptly named, since it is hard work for mother and baby. Gradually the contractions push the baby through the dilated cervix and along the vagina to the outside world. This is stage two, delivery. It is followed by stage three, afterbirth, when the placenta emerges. In practice, childbirth experiences vary. Sometimes the labour is slow, or the baby becomes stuck. Methods used to "help" the birth have ranged from the ineffectual to the barbaric. The surgical Caesarean delivery is named after Roman Emperor Julius Caesar (100-44 BC), supposedly born this way. In the past it was usually carried out if the mother died. Only this century have mother and baby had a reasonable chance. The medical speciality of childbirth is obstetrics, from the Latin *obstare*. This means to "stand opposite", referring to the midwife who stood near the mother, and helped her through the event.

MOTHER AND HER NEWBORN CHILD
The minutes and hours soon after birth are very important for mother and new baby. They quickly learn to recognize each other, particularly by scent, a sense (pp. 56-57) which is deeply rooted in the emotional parts of the brain (p. 61). The human mother-baby bond is extremely powerful, as it is even in wild animals.

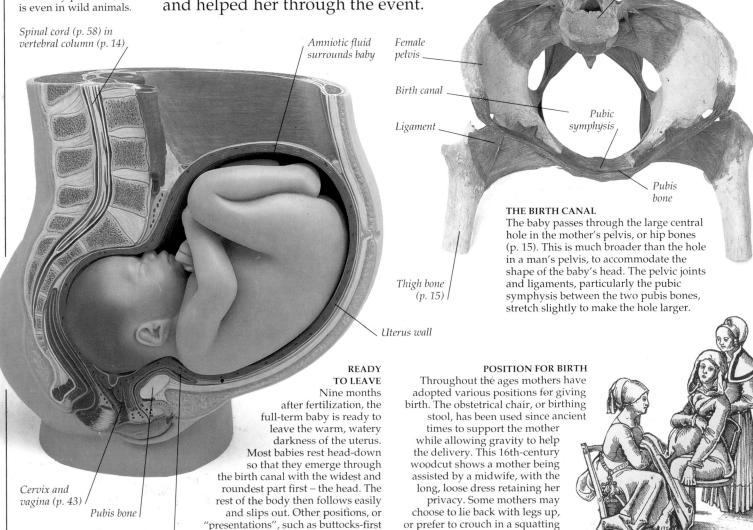

Spinal cord (p. 58) in vertebral column (p. 14)

Amniotic fluid surrounds baby

Female pelvis

Birth canal

Ligament

Vertebra (p. 14)

Pubic symphysis

Pubis bone

Thigh bone (p. 15)

Uterus wall

Cervix and vagina (p. 43)

Pubis bone

Bladder, squashed by enlarged uterus

THE BIRTH CANAL
The baby passes through the large central hole in the mother's pelvis, or hip bones (p. 15). This is much broader than the hole in a man's pelvis, to accommodate the shape of the baby's head. The pelvic joints and ligaments, particularly the pubic symphysis between the two pubis bones, stretch slightly to make the hole larger.

READY TO LEAVE
Nine months after fertilization, the full-term baby is ready to leave the warm, watery darkness of the uterus. Most babies rest head-down so that they emerge through the birth canal with the widest and roundest part first – the head. The rest of the body then follows easily and slips out. Other positions, or "presentations", such as buttocks-first (breech) or shoulder-first, are more likely to have complications.

POSITION FOR BIRTH
Throughout the ages mothers have adopted various positions for giving birth. The obstetrical chair, or birthing stool, has been used since ancient times to support the mother while allowing gravity to help the delivery. This 16th-century woodcut shows a mother being assisted by a midwife, with the long, loose dress retaining her privacy. Some mothers may choose to lie back with legs up, or prefer to crouch in a squatting position, or even give birth while floating in a pool of water.

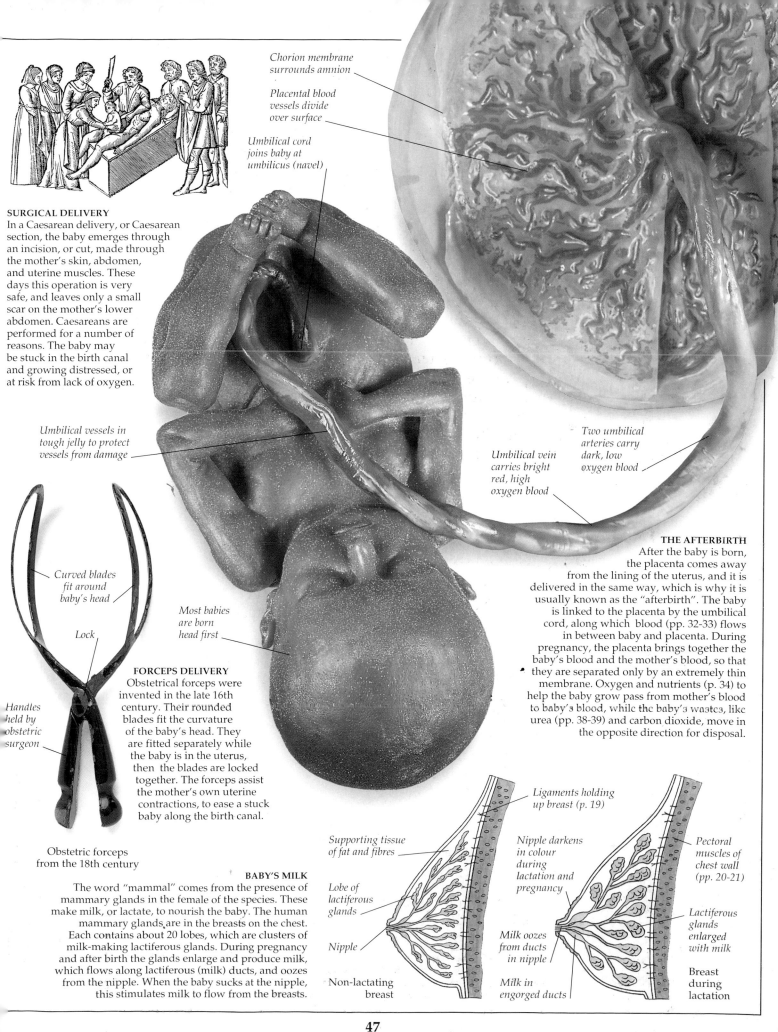

SURGICAL DELIVERY

In a Caesarean delivery, or Caesarean section, the baby emerges through an incision, or cut, made through the mother's skin, abdomen, and uterine muscles. These days this operation is very safe, and leaves only a small scar on the mother's lower abdomen. Caesareans are performed for a number of reasons. The baby may be stuck in the birth canal and growing distressed, or at risk from lack of oxygen.

Chorion membrane surrounds amnion

Placental blood vessels divide over surface

Umbilical cord joins baby at umbilicus (navel)

Umbilical vessels in tough jelly to protect vessels from damage

Umbilical vein carries bright red, high oxygen blood

Two umbilical arteries carry dark, low oxygen blood

Curved blades fit around baby's head

Lock

Most babies are born head first

Handles held by obstetric surgeon

THE AFTERBIRTH

After the baby is born, the placenta comes away from the lining of the uterus, and it is delivered in the same way, which is why it is usually known as the "afterbirth". The baby is linked to the placenta by the umbilical cord, along which blood (pp. 32-33) flows in between baby and placenta. During pregnancy, the placenta brings together the baby's blood and the mother's blood, so that they are separated only by an extremely thin membrane. Oxygen and nutrients (p. 34) to help the baby grow pass from mother's blood to baby's blood, while the baby's wastes, like urea (pp. 38-39) and carbon dioxide, move in the opposite direction for disposal.

FORCEPS DELIVERY

Obstetrical forceps were invented in the late 16th century. Their rounded blades fit the curvature of the baby's head. They are fitted separately while the baby is in the uterus, then the blades are locked together. The forceps assist the mother's own uterine contractions, to ease a stuck baby along the birth canal.

Obstetric forceps from the 18th century

BABY'S MILK

The word "mammal" comes from the presence of mammary glands in the female of the species. These make milk, or lactate, to nourish the baby. The human mammary glands are in the breasts on the chest. Each contains about 20 lobes, which are clusters of milk-making lactiferous glands. During pregnancy and after birth the glands enlarge and produce milk, which flows along lactiferous (milk) ducts, and oozes from the nipple. When the baby sucks at the nipple, this stimulates milk to flow from the breasts.

Supporting tissue of fat and fibres

Lobe of lactiferous glands

Nipple

Non-lactating breast

Ligaments holding up breast (p. 19)

Nipple darkens in colour during lactation and pregnancy

Milk oozes from ducts in nipple

Milk in engorged ducts

Pectoral muscles of chest wall (pp. 20-21)

Lactiferous glands enlarged with milk

Breast during lactation

Growth and development

NEVER AGAIN DOES THE HUMAN BODY grow so fast as it did in the womb (pp. 44-45). The single cell of the fertilized egg has multiplied billions of times. If growth continued at the same rate after birth as before, a baby would be 2 km (over 1 mile) tall by its first birthday. Throughout the first 20 years of life, the body's general pattern of growth is head-first. The brain and head lead the way, followed by the chest and abdomen, then arms and legs. A new baby has a relatively large head and short limbs. The torso catches up during childhood, and the arms and legs are the last to lengthen during the teenage years. This pattern of growth, like all of the body's physiological events, is controlled by genes. These are instructions, coded in a complex chemical form, for building and maintaining the structure and chemistry of a human being. There are 50,000-100,000 genes for a human body. Every tissue cell, such as bone, fat, or muscle, has two copies of all of them, held in the nucleus (pp. 12-13). The cells involved in reproduction – the gametes, or egg and sperm cells – have only one copy so that when they unite at fertilization, the pair is made. Red blood cells have no nucleus, and therefore do not carry genes.

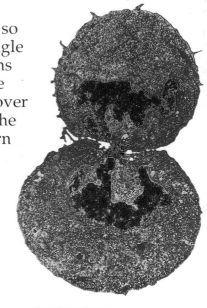

CELL DIVISION
Growth is mainly about making more cells, not bigger ones. Cells not directly involved in producing gametes for reproduction (pp. 42-43) multiply by dividing into replicas of themselves. This is known as mitosis. After a period of cell growth the genetic material, in red in this coloured electron micrograph, duplicates. The two sets of genes move apart. The outer membrane constricts, and the cell pinches itself into two separate cells.

DECIPHERING THE GENETIC CODE
Genes are made of a chemical called deoxyribonucleic acid, or DNA. This has a long, corkscrew-shaped, or helical, double molecule. Each helix carries rows of chemicals known as bases, and their varying order determines the genetic instructions. The structure was discovered by US biologist James Watson (1928-) and English biochemist Francis Crick (1916-). With Maurice Wilkins, they received a Nobel Prize in 1962.

Teeth

Teeth are specialized structures originating from bone, which undergo growth and replacement during early life. They are covered with the hardest substance in the body, enamel, which has to withstand almost a lifetime of cutting and grinding. The four different types of teeth have different roles, though these are not so marked as in mammals such as dogs and horses. Chisel-shaped incisors cut and slice; pointed canines grip and tear; broad, flat premolars and molars crush and chew.

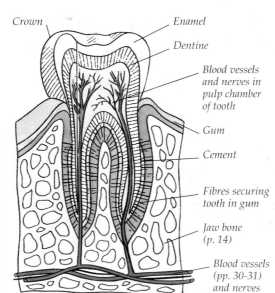

Crown
Enamel
Dentine
Blood vessels and nerves in pulp chamber of tooth
Gum
Cement
Fibres securing tooth in gum
Jaw bone (p. 14)
Blood vessels (pp. 30-31) and nerves

INSIDE A TOOTH
The crown of the tooth, exposed above the gum, is anchored by long roots, glued by living "cement" into the jaw bone. Under the incredibly hard enamel is slightly softer, shock-absorbing dentine, to make chewing more comfortable. Within this is the pulp chamber, containing blood vessels that nourish the living tooth, and nerves (pp. 58-59) that warn of injury, disease, or decay.

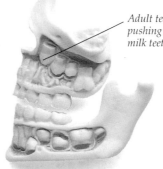

Jaw is cut away to reveal teeth
Tooth buds growing in jaw bone

BIRTH DAY TEETH
A newborn baby's teeth are usually hidden below the gums. They become visible, or erupt, from the age of about six months.

Adult teeth pushing out milk teeth

FIVE-YEAR TEETH
The first 20 teeth to grow are called the primary, deciduous, or milk teeth. From about six years these begin to fall out, and the adult set grows in their place.

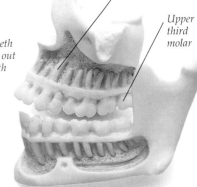

Tooth roots in jaw
Upper third molar

FULL SET OF ADULT TEETH
By 21 years of age, all 32 teeth are usually through. In each side of each jaw are two incisors, one canine, two premolars, and three molars. In some people the third molars never erupt.

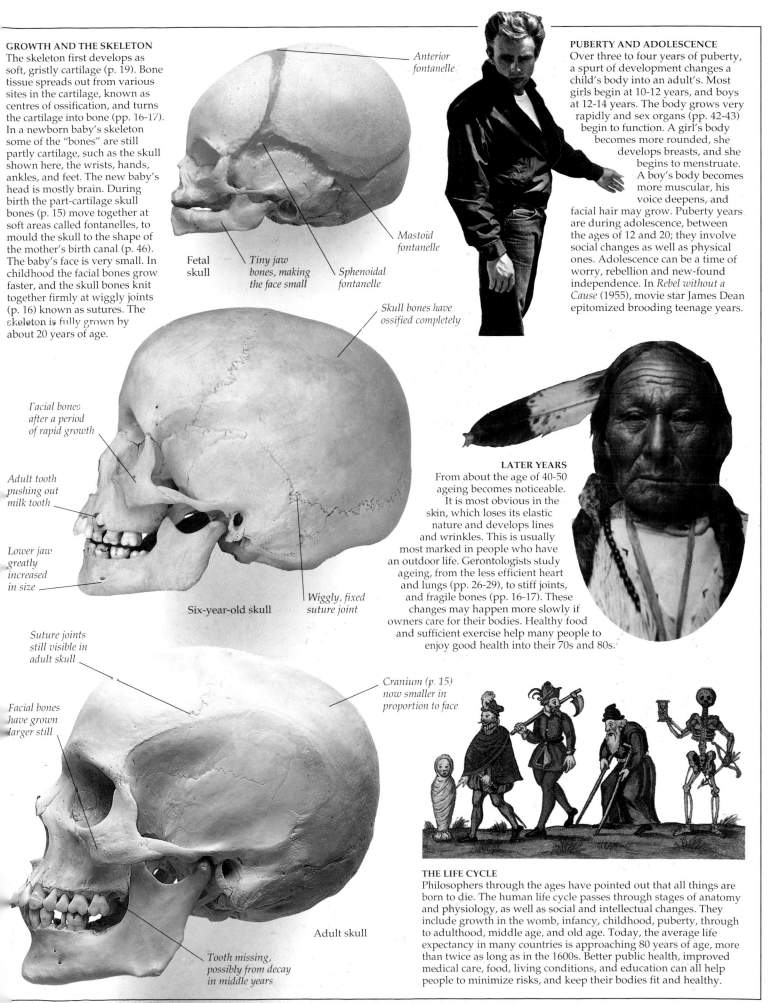

GROWTH AND THE SKELETON

The skeleton first develops as soft, gristly cartilage (p. 19). Bone tissue spreads out from various sites in the cartilage, known as centres of ossification, and turns the cartilage into bone (pp. 16-17). In a newborn baby's skeleton some of the "bones" are still partly cartilage, such as the skull shown here, the wrists, hands, ankles, and feet. The new baby's head is mostly brain. During birth the part-cartilage skull bones (p. 15) move together at soft areas called fontanelles, to mould the skull to the shape of the mother's birth canal (p. 46). The baby's face is very small. In childhood the facial bones grow faster, and the skull bones knit together firmly at wiggly joints (p. 16) known as sutures. The skeleton is fully grown by about 20 years of age.

Anterior fontanelle

Mastoid fontanelle

Sphenoidal fontanelle

Fetal skull

Tiny jaw bones, making the face small

Skull bones have ossified completely

Facial bones after a period of rapid growth

Adult tooth pushing out milk tooth

Lower jaw greatly increased in size

Six-year-old skull

Wiggly, fixed suture joint

Suture joints still visible in adult skull

Facial bones have grown larger still

Cranium (p. 15) now smaller in proportion to face

Adult skull

Tooth missing, possibly from decay in middle years

PUBERTY AND ADOLESCENCE

Over three to four years of puberty, a spurt of development changes a child's body into an adult's. Most girls begin at 10-12 years, and boys at 12-14 years. The body grows very rapidly and sex organs (pp. 42-43) begin to function. A girl's body becomes more rounded, she develops breasts, and she begins to menstruate. A boy's body becomes more muscular, his voice deepens, and facial hair may grow. Puberty years are during adolescence, between the ages of 12 and 20; they involve social changes as well as physical ones. Adolescence can be a time of worry, rebellion and new-found independence. In *Rebel without a Cause* (1955), movie star James Dean epitomized brooding teenage years.

LATER YEARS

From about the age of 40-50 ageing becomes noticeable. It is most obvious in the skin, which loses its elastic nature and develops lines and wrinkles. This is usually most marked in people who have an outdoor life. Gerontologists study ageing, from the less efficient heart and lungs (pp. 26-29), to stiff joints, and fragile bones (pp. 16-17). These changes may happen more slowly if owners care for their bodies. Healthy food and sufficient exercise help many people to enjoy good health into their 70s and 80s.

THE LIFE CYCLE

Philosophers through the ages have pointed out that all things are born to die. The human life cycle passes through stages of anatomy and physiology, as well as social and intellectual changes. They include growth in the womb, infancy, childhood, puberty, through to adulthood, middle age, and old age. Today, the average life expectancy in many countries is approaching 80 years of age, more than twice as long as in the 1600s. Better public health, improved medical care, food, living conditions, and education can all help people to minimize risks, and keep their bodies fit and healthy.

Skin and touch

ARISTOTLE OF ANCIENT GREECE listed the five main senses as sight, hearing, smell, taste, and touch. Unlike the other sense organs, the body part involved in touch is not concerned with sense alone. It has many other functions. Indeed it is the body's biggest organ – the skin. On an adult, this living, leathery overcoat weighs about 5 kg (11 lb) and has an area of some 2 sq m (2.4 sq yd). Its tough surface layer, the epidermis, continually replaces itself in order to repair wear and tear, and keeps out water, dust, germs, and harmful rays like ultraviolet from the sun. Under this is a thicker layer, the dermis, packed with nerves, blood vessels, and stringy fibres of the body proteins, collagen and elastin. The dermis also assists in temperature regulation, by sweating (p. 39), and turning pale or flushed. Skin was ignored by many great anatomists. They dismissed it as something to be removed in order to study the more interesting bits beneath. Like many other body parts, the invention of the microscope made the skin's fascinating details visible.

FRICTION RIDGES
The epidermal skin layer of the fingers, palms, soles, and toes is folded and tucked into swirling patterns of ridges. Each ridge is about 0.2-0.4 mm (0.008-0.016 in) wide. Along with the slight dampness from sweat and oil-producing sebaceous glands, the ridges help the skin to grip without slippage. On the fingers, these are called fingerprints. They are classified into types by the presence of three main features: arches, loops, and whorls. Each human has its own unique set of fingerprints.

FINGERTIP READING
Braille and other touch-reading systems help people with limited eyesight. Fingertip skin is sensitive enough to detect patterns of raised dots representing numbers and letters. French inventor Louis Braille (1809-1852) was blinded when three years old, and began to devise his system from the age of 15 years.

UNDER THE SKIN
The surface of the skin is dead. It consists of flat, interlocking dead cells, filled with the hard-wearing protein keratin. These wear away and are replaced by cells moving up from below, like a conveyor belt. The cells are produced by continual division (p. 48) at the base of the skin's upper layer, the epidermis. The dermis is much thicker, and contains various microscopic sensors responsible for touch – which is a combination of light pressure, heavy pressure, heat, cold, and pain. The dermis houses about 3 million tiny coiled sweat glands (p. 39), and roughly as many hair follicles, from which hairs grow.

Merkel's disc

Hair shaft

Outer layer is the epidermis

Meissner's corpuscle, touch nerve ending

Middle layer is the dermis

Sebaceous gland produces oil to waterproof the skin

Blood vessels supplying the skin

Pacinian corpuscle

Inner layer, the hypodermis, contains fatty tissue

Hair follicle

Sweat gland

Dermis

Melanin stained black

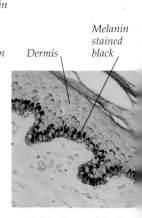

Light micrograph of skin, showing presence of melanin

DEAD HAIRS
In this scanning electron micrograph, hairs protrude from their pit-like follicles in the skin. Only the base of the hair, where it grows, is alive. The shaft that shows above the surface is, like the skin around it, made chiefly of keratin and quite dead. There are some 100,000 hairs on the average head. Each head hair grows at the rate of 1 mm (0.04 in) every three or four days. There are also much tinier hairs over the rest of the body. The only hairless skin is on the palms of the hands, the palm-sides of the fingers, and the soles of the feet.

SKIN COLOUR DIFFERENCES
One of the differences between humans and other primates is the much smaller, finer hairs covering the body, so that humans look almost hairless compared to monkeys and apes. Thus humans have less protection from the Sun's ultraviolet rays, which could damage the skin and the tissues underneath. The presence of melanin, a dark brown pigment made by cells in the skin, protects the tissues beneath from the Sun's rays. As humans moved to more temperate regions, having lots of pigment became less important.

Sun-damaged skin, due to lack of melanin

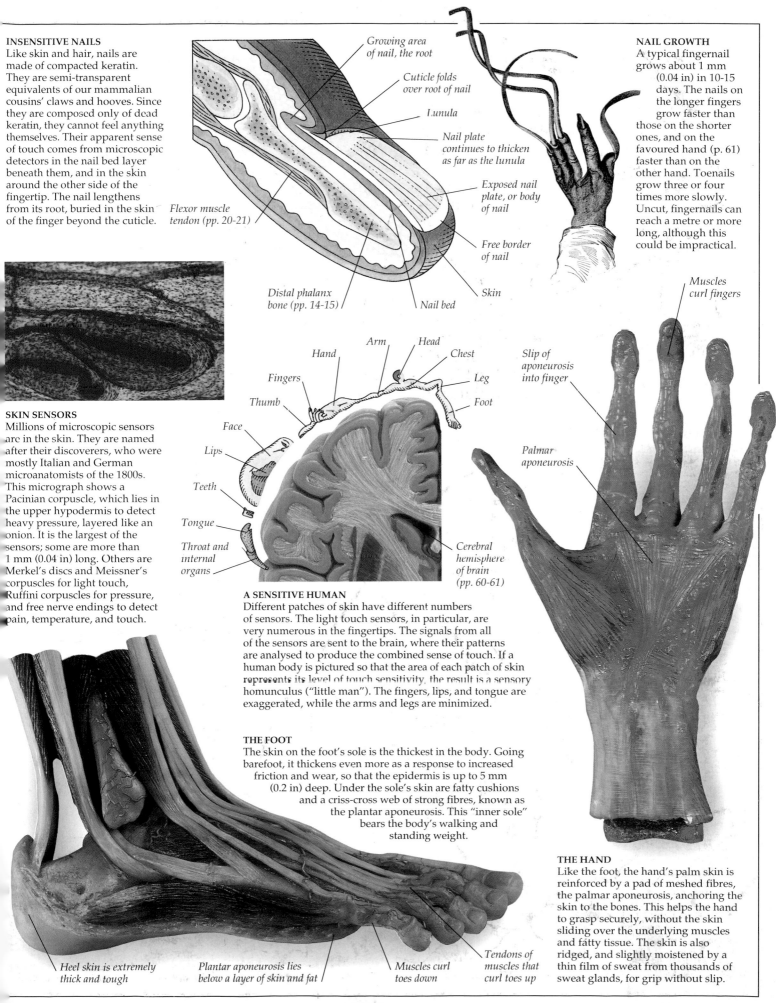

INSENSITIVE NAILS

Like skin and hair, nails are made of compacted keratin. They are semi-transparent equivalents of our mammalian cousins' claws and hooves. Since they are composed only of dead keratin, they cannot feel anything themselves. Their apparent sense of touch comes from microscopic detectors in the nail bed layer beneath them, and in the skin around the other side of the fingertip. The nail lengthens from its root, buried in the skin of the finger beyond the cuticle.

Growing area of nail, the root

Cuticle folds over root of nail

Lunula

Nail plate continues to thicken as far as the lunula

Exposed nail plate, or body of nail

Free border of nail

Skin

Flexor muscle tendon (pp. 20-21)

Distal phalanx bone (pp. 14-15)

Nail bed

NAIL GROWTH

A typical fingernail grows about 1 mm (0.04 in) in 10-15 days. The nails on the longer fingers grow faster than those on the shorter ones, and on the favoured hand (p. 61) faster than on the other hand. Toenails grow three or four times more slowly. Uncut, fingernails can reach a metre or more long, although this could be impractical.

Muscles curl fingers

Slip of aponeurosis into finger

Palmar aponeurosis

SKIN SENSORS

Millions of microscopic sensors are in the skin. They are named after their discoverers, who were mostly Italian and German microanatomists of the 1800s. This micrograph shows a Pacinian corpuscle, which lies in the upper hypodermis to detect heavy pressure, layered like an onion. It is the largest of the sensors; some are more than 1 mm (0.04 in) long. Others are Merkel's discs and Meissner's corpuscles for light touch, Ruffini corpuscles for pressure, and free nerve endings to detect pain, temperature, and touch.

Hand · *Arm* · *Head* · *Chest* · *Leg* · *Foot*

Fingers

Thumb

Face

Lips

Teeth

Tongue

Throat and internal organs

Cerebral hemisphere of brain (pp. 60-61)

A SENSITIVE HUMAN

Different patches of skin have different numbers of sensors. The light touch sensors, in particular, are very numerous in the fingertips. The signals from all of the sensors are sent to the brain, where their patterns are analysed to produce the combined sense of touch. If a human body is pictured so that the area of each patch of skin represents its level of touch sensitivity, the result is a sensory homunculus ("little man"). The fingers, lips, and tongue are exaggerated, while the arms and legs are minimized.

THE FOOT

The skin on the foot's sole is the thickest in the body. Going barefoot, it thickens even more as a response to increased friction and wear, so that the epidermis is up to 5 mm (0.2 in) deep. Under the sole's skin are fatty cushions and a criss-cross web of strong fibres, known as the plantar aponeurosis. This "inner sole" bears the body's walking and standing weight.

Heel skin is extremely thick and tough

Plantar aponeurosis lies below a layer of skin and fat

Muscles curl toes down

Tendons of muscles that curl toes up

THE HAND

Like the foot, the hand's palm skin is reinforced by a pad of meshed fibres, the palmar aponeurosis, anchoring the skin to the bones. This helps the hand to grasp securely, without the skin sliding over the underlying muscles and fatty tissue. The skin is also ridged, and slightly moistened by a thin film of sweat from thousands of sweat glands, for grip without slip.

Eyes and seeing

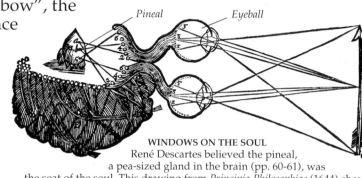

CROSS-EYED
An Arabic drawing, nearly 1,000 years old, shows the optic nerves crossing. Half of the nerve fibres from the right eye actually pass to the left side of the brain, and vice versa.

THE BODY ACTUALLY HAS MORE than just five senses of sight, hearing, smell, taste, and touch. Sensors around the body can detect temperature, positions of body parts such as muscles and joints, and levels of oxygen, nutrients, and other chemicals in body fluids. The main sense is sight. Two-thirds of the mind's conscious attention is taken up by what the eyes see, and two-thirds of information stored in the brain has come in by vision – as pictures, words, and other visual means. At Alexandria in the first century AD, the anatomist Rufus of Ephesus described the main parts of the eye: the dome-like cornea at the front, the coloured iris, or "rainbow", the lens (named from its resemblance to a lentil), and the vitreous humour, or "glassy fluid" inside the eyeball. Only with the microscope (pp. 12-13) could anatomists see the millions of rod and cone cells in the retina, which is the thin layer on the inside of the eyeball. These cells detect light rays, turn them into nerve signals, which the optic nerve transmits to the brain for interpretation into images.

Pineal   *Eyeball*

WINDOWS ON THE SOUL
René Descartes believed the pineal, a pea-sized gland in the brain (pp. 60-61), was the seat of the soul. This drawing from *Principia Philosophiae* (1644) shows his mistaken theory that "animal spirit" carrying visual information passed from the eyes along hollow optic nerves, directly to the pineal.

OUTSIDE THE EYE
The wall of the eyeball is a three-layered sandwich. Outermost is the sclera, pale and tough, and visible at the front as the "white" of the eye. In the middle is the choroid, dark and spongy, and rich in blood vessels. The innermost layer is the light-detecting retina ("net"). Tissue-thin, with a working area hardly bigger than a thumbnail, it detects an incredibly detailed, full-colour view of the world.

Sclera

Choroid

Pupil   *Iris*

Lens   *Retina*   *Vitreous humour within body of eyeball*

Cornea   *Optic nerve*

Choroid

Sclera

INSIDE THE EYE
The clear cornea at the front of the eye is covered by a very thin layer, the conjunctiva. Behind the cornea is the iris, a coloured ring of muscles around a hole in its centre, the pupil. The ring automatically widens in bright light to reduce the size of the pupil, protecting the eye's delicate retina from too much potentially damaging light.

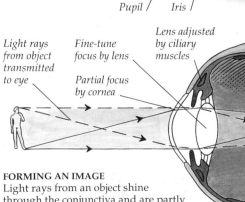

Light rays from object transmitted to eye

Fine-tune focus by lens

Lens adjusted by ciliary muscles

Partial focus by cornea

Upside-down image formed at back of retina

Optic nerve

Muscle to rotate eyeball

FORMING AN IMAGE
Light rays from an object shine through the conjunctiva and are partly focused by the cornea. They pass through the pupil, are focused further by the lens, pass through the vitreous humour, and form an image on the retina. Because of the way lenses work, the image is upside down, and the brain turns it "right way up". The ciliary muscles adjust the lens' shape, making it fatter to focus nearby objects clearly on to the retina.

THE "SEEING" CELLS
The electron microscope reveals two kinds of light-detecting cells in the retina. The rods (purple) "see" only in shades of grey, but they respond well in dim light. The cones (blue) are mainly at the back of the retina and see details and colours, but work well only in bright light. Each eye has about 120 million rods and 6 or 7 million cones.

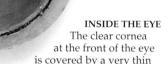

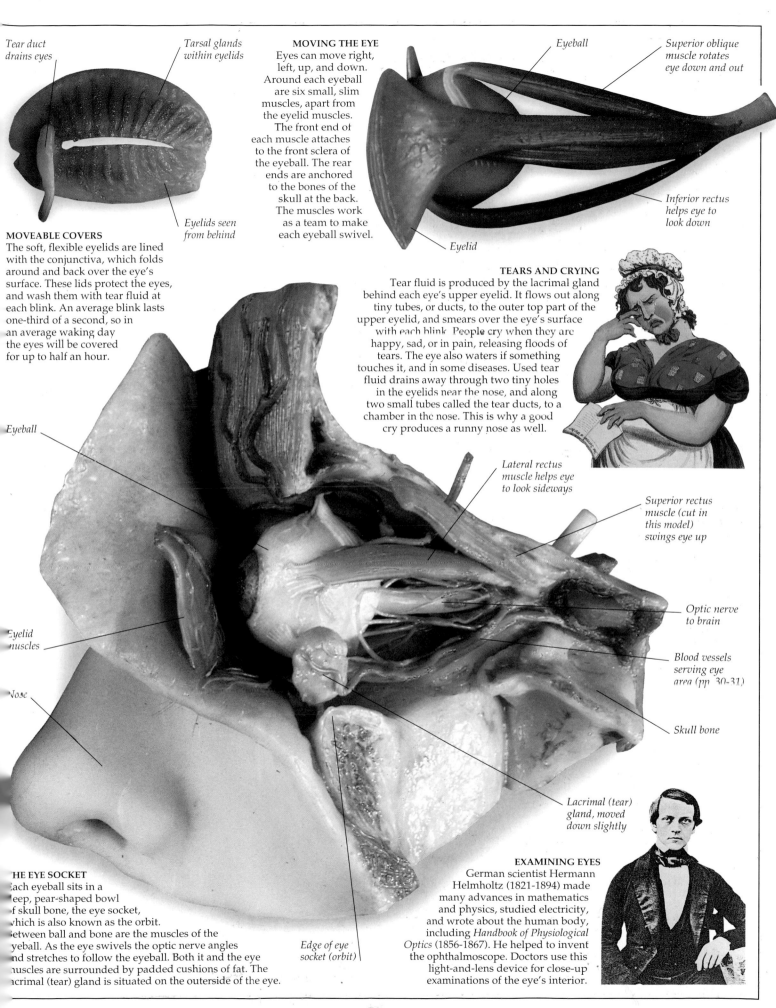

Tear duct drains eyes

Tarsal glands within eyelids

MOVING THE EYE
Eyes can move right, left, up, and down. Around each eyeball are six small, slim muscles, apart from the eyelid muscles. The front end of each muscle attaches to the front sclera of the eyeball. The rear ends are anchored to the bones of the skull at the back. The muscles work as a team to make each eyeball swivel.

Eyeball

Superior oblique muscle rotates eye down and out

Inferior rectus helps eye to look down

Eyelids seen from behind

Eyelid

MOVEABLE COVERS
The soft, flexible eyelids are lined with the conjunctiva, which folds around and back over the eye's surface. These lids protect the eyes, and wash them with tear fluid at each blink. An average blink lasts one-third of a second, so in an average waking day the eyes will be covered for up to half an hour.

TEARS AND CRYING
Tear fluid is produced by the lacrimal gland behind each eye's upper eyelid. It flows out along tiny tubes, or ducts, to the outer top part of the upper eyelid, and smears over the eye's surface with each blink. People cry when they are happy, sad, or in pain, releasing floods of tears. The eye also waters if something touches it, and in some diseases. Used tear fluid drains away through two tiny holes in the eyelids near the nose, and along two small tubes called the tear ducts, to a chamber in the nose. This is why a good cry produces a runny nose as well.

Eyeball

Lateral rectus muscle helps eye to look sideways

Superior rectus muscle (cut in this model) swings eye up

Eyelid muscles

Optic nerve to brain

Blood vessels serving eye area (pp. 30-31)

Nose

Skull bone

Lacrimal (tear) gland, moved down slightly

THE EYE SOCKET
Each eyeball sits in a deep, pear-shaped bowl of skull bone, the eye socket, which is also known as the orbit. Between ball and bone are the muscles of the eyeball. As the eye swivels the optic nerve angles and stretches to follow the eyeball. Both it and the eye muscles are surrounded by padded cushions of fat. The lacrimal (tear) gland is situated on the outside of the eye.

Edge of eye socket (orbit)

EXAMINING EYES
German scientist Hermann Helmholtz (1821-1894) made many advances in mathematics and physics, studied electricity, and wrote about the human body, including *Handbook of Physiological Optics* (1856-1867). He helped to invent the ophthalmoscope. Doctors use this light-and-lens device for close-up examinations of the eye's interior.

Ears and hearing

AFTER SIGHT, HEARING IS THE SENSE that provides the brain with most information about the outside world. Compared with other animals, the human ear registers a fairly wide range of sounds. These vary in volume from the delicate notes of a flute to the ear-splitting chords of a heavy-metal electric guitar. They vary in pitch from the deep thunderous roar of a jet engine to the high trills of bird song. Ears did not figure greatly in the writings of ancients such as Aristotle of Greece and Galen of Rome. The Egyptians knew that ears heard, but they also thought that ears were involved in breathing.

The scientific study of hearing began in earnest in the 1500s. *The Examination of the Organ of Hearing*, published in 1562, was probably the first major work devoted to ears. Its author was Bartolomeo Eustachio (1520-1574). His name lives on in the eustachian tube, or the pharyngo-tympanic tube, that connects the air-filled middle ear cavity to the back of the throat.

THE MIND'S EAR
One of the all-time musical greats, Ludwig van Beethoven (1770-1827), noticed deafness approaching before his 30th birthday. He resolved to defy his handicap and composed some of his finest works – by hearing the notes in his head.

ECLIPSED BY VESALIUS
Eustachio studied as a professor in Rome, at around the same time that Andreas Vesalius was revolutionizing anatomy in Padua. His book on the ear covers several parts that were already known, including the tube now named after him. This had been described almost 2,000 years previously by a physician of Greece, Alcmaeon of Croton.

INSIDE THE EAR
Italian mini- and microanatomist Antonio Valsalva (1666-1723) updated and expanded Eustachio's book with his own *On the Human Ear* in 1704. He was the first to recognize the ear has three main parts. The outer ear consists of the ear flap and the auditory canal. The middle ear contains the eardrum and three tiny bones, the ossicles. The inner ear comprises the snail-shaped cochlea, semicircular canals, and other fluid-filled chambers.

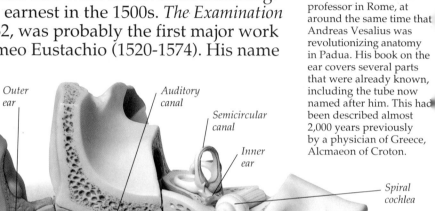

Outer ear

Auditory canal

Semicircular canal

Inner ear

Spiral cochlea

Temporal bone of skull

Eustachian tube to throat

Right ear flap

Eardrum

Middle ear

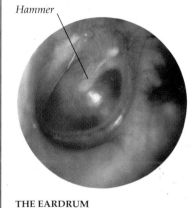

Hammer

THE EARDRUM
This taut membrane, like stretched skin, is slightly smaller than a little finger's nail. It marks the divide between the outer ear and the middle ear. It can be seen directly or photographed by placing a medical instrument, the otoscope, into the auditory canal. Through the eardrum is a hazy view of the first of the ear ossicles, the hammer. The "handle" of the hammer is firmly attached across half of the eardrum.

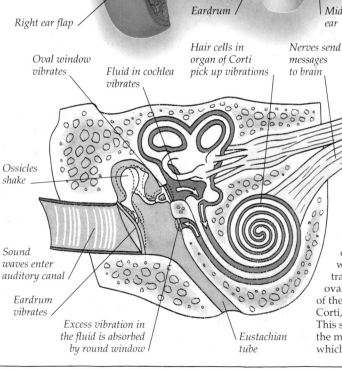

Oval window vibrates

Fluid in cochlea vibrates

Hair cells in organ of Corti pick up vibrations

Nerves send messages to brain

Vestibular nerve

Cochlear nerve

Ossicles shake

Sound waves enter auditory canal

Eardrum vibrates

Excess vibration in the fluid is absorbed by round window

Eustachian tube

HEARING
Airborne sound waves funnel into the auditory canal and strike the eardrum, making it vibrate back and forth. These vibrations pass along the three tiny ear ossicles linked by miniature joints (pp. 18-19) which shake in turn. The third ossicle transfers the vibration through the flexible oval window into the fluid of the cochlea. Parts of the cochlea's membrane, in the spiral organ of Corti, shake in sympathy with the vibrations. This shaking pulls microscopic hairs on cells in the membrane, which generates nerve signals, which flash along the cochlear nerve to the brain.

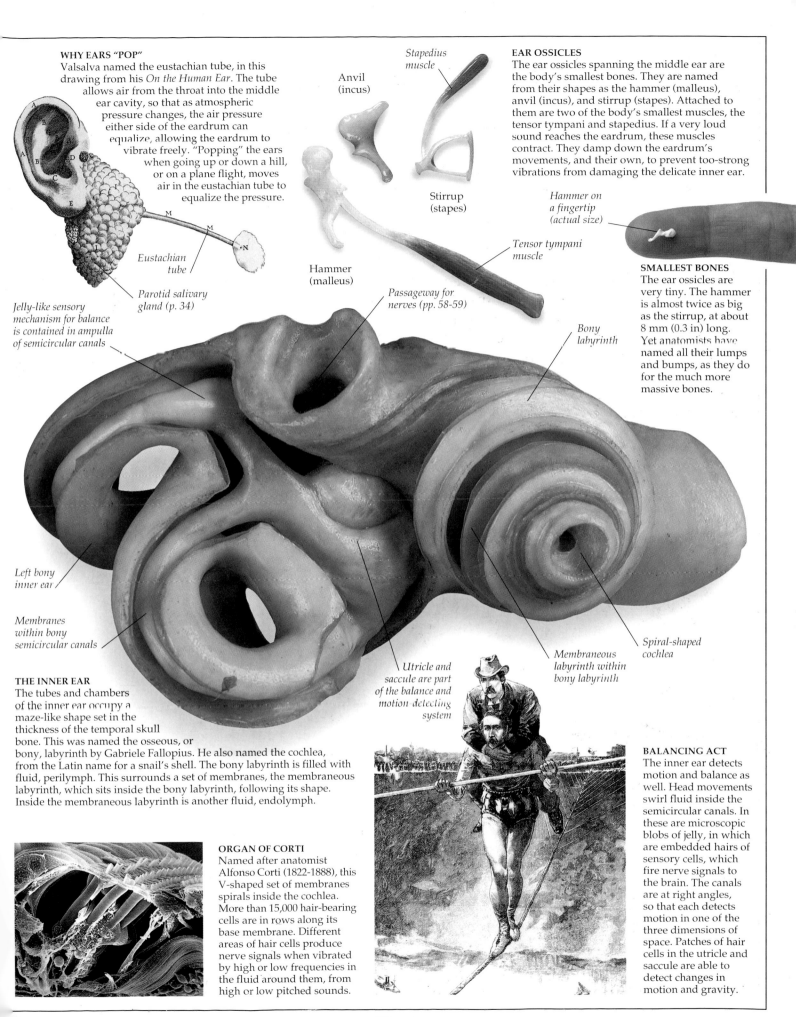

WHY EARS "POP"

Valsalva named the eustachian tube, in this drawing from his *On the Human Ear*. The tube allows air from the throat into the middle ear cavity, so that as atmospheric pressure changes, the air pressure either side of the eardrum can equalize, allowing the eardrum to vibrate freely. "Popping" the ears when going up or down a hill, or on a plane flight, moves air in the eustachian tube to equalize the pressure.

Eustachian tube

Parotid salivary gland (p. 34)

Stapedius muscle

Anvil (incus)

Stirrup (stapes)

Hammer (malleus)

EAR OSSICLES

The ear ossicles spanning the middle ear are the body's smallest bones. They are named from their shapes as the hammer (malleus), anvil (incus), and stirrup (stapes). Attached to them are two of the body's smallest muscles, the tensor tympani and stapedius. If a very loud sound reaches the eardrum, these muscles contract. They damp down the eardrum's movements, and their own, to prevent too-strong vibrations from damaging the delicate inner ear.

Hammer on a fingertip (actual size)

Tensor tympani muscle

SMALLEST BONES

The ear ossicles are very tiny. The hammer is almost twice as big as the stirrup, at about 8 mm (0.3 in) long. Yet anatomists have named all their lumps and bumps, as they do for the much more massive bones.

Jelly-like sensory mechanism for balance is contained in ampulla of semicircular canals

Passageway for nerves (pp. 58-59)

Bony labyrinth

Left bony inner ear

Membranes within bony semicircular canals

Utricle and saccule are part of the balance and motion-detecting system

Membraneous labyrinth within bony labyrinth

Spiral-shaped cochlea

THE INNER EAR

The tubes and chambers of the inner ear occupy a maze-like shape set in the thickness of the temporal skull bone. This was named the osseous, or bony, labyrinth by Gabriele Fallopius. He also named the cochlea, from the Latin name for a snail's shell. The bony labyrinth is filled with fluid, perilymph. This surrounds a set of membranes, the membraneous labyrinth, which sits inside the bony labyrinth, following its shape. Inside the membraneous labyrinth is another fluid, endolymph.

ORGAN OF CORTI

Named after anatomist Alfonso Corti (1822-1888), this V-shaped set of membranes spirals inside the cochlea. More than 15,000 hair-bearing cells are in rows along its base membrane. Different areas of hair cells produce nerve signals when vibrated by high or low frequencies in the fluid around them, from high or low pitched sounds.

BALANCING ACT

The inner ear detects motion and balance as well. Head movements swirl fluid inside the semicircular canals. In these are microscopic blobs of jelly, in which are embedded hairs of sensory cells, which fire nerve signals to the brain. The canals are at right angles, so that each detects motion in one of the three dimensions of space. Patches of hair cells in the utricle and saccule are able to detect changes in motion and gravity.

Smell and taste

IN COMMON WITH OTHER MAMMALS, the human body has senses of taste and smell to monitor nutrients going into the digestive system. Poisonous, rotting, or unfamiliar foods and drinks produce foul smells and sharp tastes, which warn against eating or drinking. Smell is also an early-warning system for tainted air, smoke, and other dangers. These senses are often a source of pleasure as well as warning. Smell, or olfaction, detects the scents of herbs, spices, and perfumes, and taste, or gustation, picks out the flavours of a good meal. Smell and taste are known as the chemical senses, or chemosenses. The nose and tongue detect molecules of certain chemicals, either odour molecules floating in the air or flavour molecules in food and drink. The presence of the chemicals triggers sensors on microscopic cells in the nose's roof and on the tongue's surface. The cells make nerve signals that travel to the brain for analysis by its smell and taste centres. When eating and drinking, smell and taste work closely together to produce the sensory impressions of the meal.

MALODOROUS AIR
For centuries, physicians suspected that diseases could spread by foul smells. For example, malaria means "bad air" in Italian. This Middle Ages physician holds a pomander – a sachet of aromatic herbs – to his nose. As well as masking the stench, the pomander was thought to protect the physician against the risk of catching the patient's ailment, in this case the Black Death.

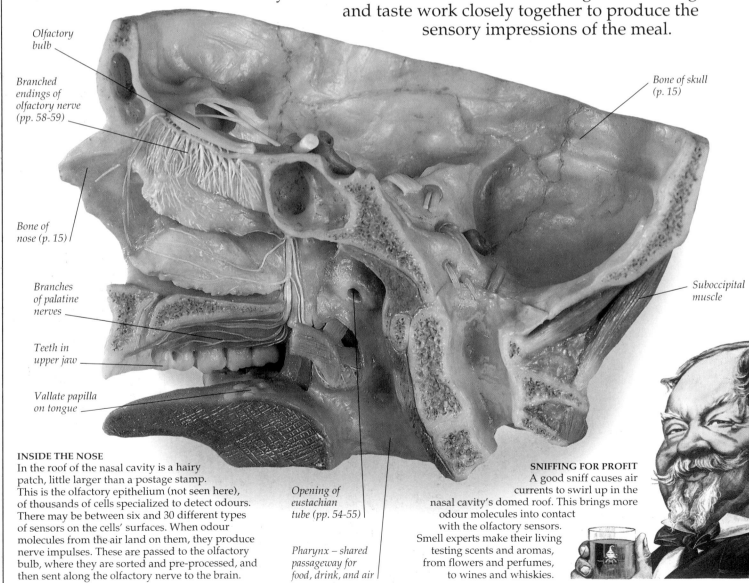

Olfactory bulb

Branched endings of olfactory nerve (pp. 58-59)

Bone of nose (p. 15)

Branches of palatine nerves

Teeth in upper jaw

Vallate papilla on tongue

Bone of skull (p. 15)

Suboccipital muscle

Opening of eustachian tube (pp. 54-55)

Pharynx – shared passageway for food, drink, and air

INSIDE THE NOSE
In the roof of the nasal cavity is a hairy patch, little larger than a postage stamp. This is the olfactory epithelium (not seen here), of thousands of cells specialized to detect odours. There may be between six and 30 different types of sensors on the cells' surfaces. When odour molecules from the air land on them, they produce nerve impulses. These are passed to the olfactory bulb, where they are sorted and pre-processed, and then sent along the olfactory nerve to the brain.

SNIFFING FOR PROFIT
A good sniff causes air currents to swirl up in the nasal cavity's domed roof. This brings more odour molecules into contact with the olfactory sensors. Smell experts make their living testing scents and aromas, from flowers and perfumes, to wines and whiskies.

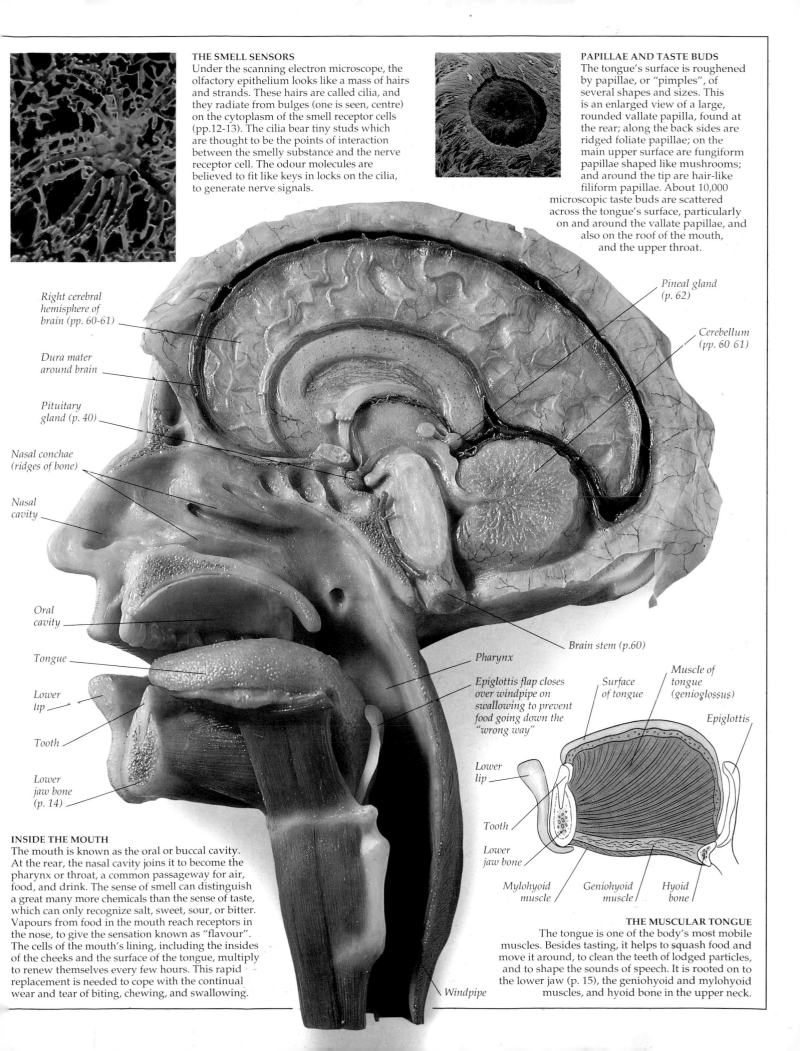

THE SMELL SENSORS

Under the scanning electron microscope, the olfactory epithelium looks like a mass of hairs and strands. These hairs are called cilia, and they radiate from bulges (one is seen, centre) on the cytoplasm of the smell receptor cells (pp.12-13). The cilia bear tiny studs which are thought to be the points of interaction between the smelly substance and the nerve receptor cell. The odour molecules are believed to fit like keys in locks on the cilia, to generate nerve signals.

PAPILLAE AND TASTE BUDS

The tongue's surface is roughened by papillae, or "pimples", of several shapes and sizes. This is an enlarged view of a large, rounded vallate papilla, found at the rear; along the back sides are ridged foliate papillae; on the main upper surface are fungiform papillae shaped like mushrooms; and around the tip are hair-like filiform papillae. About 10,000 microscopic taste buds are scattered across the tongue's surface, particularly on and around the vallate papillae, and also on the roof of the mouth, and the upper throat.

Right cerebral hemisphere of brain (pp. 60-61)

Dura mater around brain

Pituitary gland (p. 40)

Nasal conchae (ridges of bone)

Nasal cavity

Oral cavity

Tongue

Lower lip

Tooth

Lower jaw bone (p. 14)

Pineal gland (p. 62)

Cerebellum (pp. 60 61)

Brain stem (p.60)

Pharynx

Epiglottis flap closes over windpipe on swallowing to prevent food going down the "wrong way"

Windpipe

Surface of tongue

Muscle of tongue (genioglossus)

Epiglottis

Lower lip

Tooth

Lower jaw bone

Mylohyoid muscle

Geniohyoid muscle

Hyoid bone

INSIDE THE MOUTH

The mouth is known as the oral or buccal cavity. At the rear, the nasal cavity joins it to become the pharynx or throat, a common passageway for air, food, and drink. The sense of smell can distinguish a great many more chemicals than the sense of taste, which can only recognize salt, sweet, sour, or bitter. Vapours from food in the mouth reach receptors in the nose, to give the sensation known as "flavour". The cells of the mouth's lining, including the insides of the cheeks and the surface of the tongue, multiply to renew themselves every few hours. This rapid replacement is needed to cope with the continual wear and tear of biting, chewing, and swallowing.

THE MUSCULAR TONGUE

The tongue is one of the body's most mobile muscles. Besides tasting, it helps to squash food and move it around, to clean the teeth of lodged particles, and to shape the sounds of speech. It is rooted on to the lower jaw (p. 15), the geniohyoid and mylohyoid muscles, and hyoid bone in the upper neck.

The nervous system

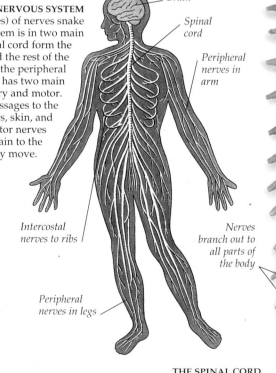

Spinal cord continues up to brain stem (pp. 60-61)

WITHOUT ITS TELEPHONE SYSTEM of cables, snaking across the land and spreading through towns and cities, a modern country would soon be paralysed. Without its nervous system, so would the body. Nerves are the communication network of the body. They carry messages to and fro, inform, and coordinate. Like telephone signals, nerve signals are electrical, though they are only about one-twentieth of a volt in strength. Herophilus at Alexandria was the first to notice that nerves were concerned with sensations and movements, in around 300 BC. Roman anatomist Galen recognized the nerves' roles in control and coordination, but he thought that nerves were hollow and some type of mystical "animal spirit" fluid passed through them. His mistaken theories influenced science, and held back progress for a further 15 centuries. Vesalius mapped the nervous system, but not in his usual detail. However, he did show that nipping the end of an exposed nerve would cause the muscle attached to jump. With the discovery of the electrical nature of nerve signals in the late 1700s, the workings of the nervous system were at last becoming clearer.

A WARNING SIGN
Microscopic and tree-like, nerve endings are found in the skin and in many internal organs. They register discomfort and pain, from a broken bone to an aching tooth – or a pulled tooth. Pain warns that something is amiss, and action should be taken to care for the body.

"ANIMAL ELECTRICITY"
Anatomist Luigi Galvani (1737-1798) of Bologna noticed that an isolated frog's leg twitched when metallic contact was made between its nerve and its muscle. He believed the nerves contained "animal electricity". Physicist and rival Alessandro Volta (1745-1827) showed the electrical nature of the nerve signal.

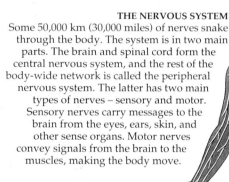

THE NERVOUS SYSTEM
Some 50,000 km (30,000 miles) of nerves snake through the body. The system is in two main parts. The brain and spinal cord form the central nervous system, and the rest of the body-wide network is called the peripheral nervous system. The latter has two main types of nerves – sensory and motor. Sensory nerves carry messages to the brain from the eyes, ears, skin, and other sense organs. Motor nerves convey signals from the brain to the muscles, making the body move.

Brain

Spinal cord

Peripheral nerves in arm

Intercostal nerves to ribs

Nerves branch out to all parts of the body

Peripheral nerves in legs

PAVLOV'S PERFORMING DOGS
A reflex is an automatic reaction, carried out by nerve signals. An example is when dogs naturally salivate, or drool, at the sight and smell of a meal. Conducting experiments on the digestive system, scientist Ivan Pavlov of Russia (1849-1936) noted that dogs salivated at the sight of their handler, even without food. He trained them to associate food with the sound of the bell. After a time they drooled upon hearing the bell alone. This type of "re-programmed" auto-action is known as a conditioned reflex.

THE SPINAL CORD
The spinal cord is, in effect, a downward extension of the brain. It is well protected from damage by knocks, kinks, and pressure, lying inside the long tunnel formed by the holes through the vertebrae, or backbones (pp. 14-15). From its 40-cm (16-in) length branch 31 pairs of nerves, each carrying signals to and from a certain part of both sides of the body.

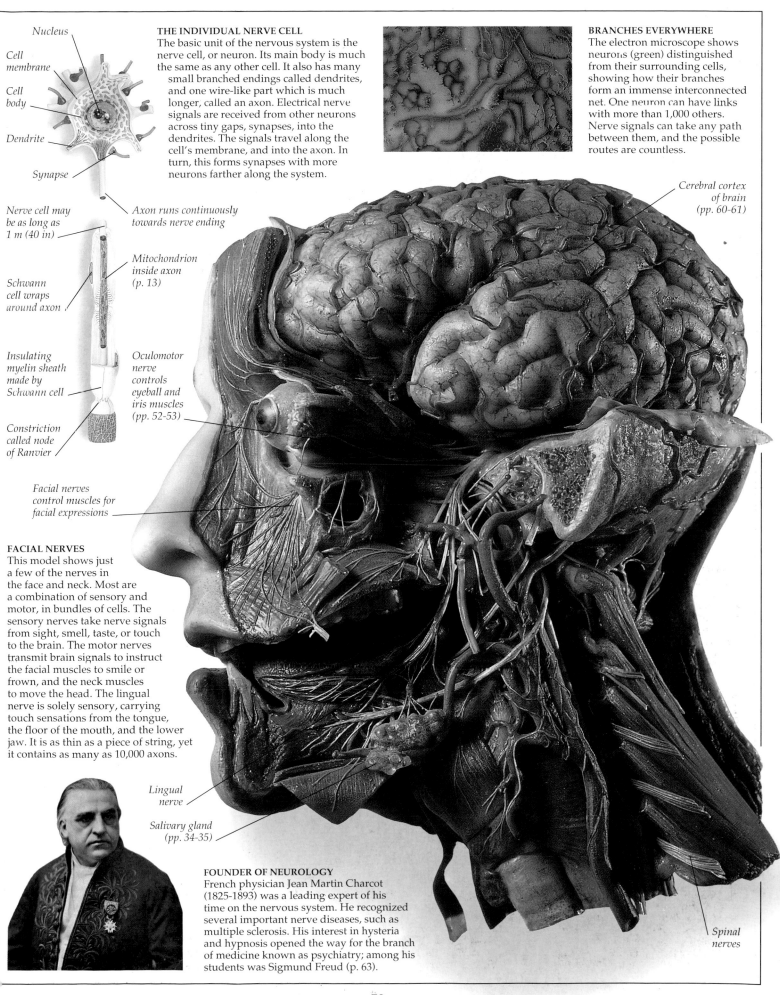

THE INDIVIDUAL NERVE CELL
The basic unit of the nervous system is the nerve cell, or neuron. Its main body is much the same as any other cell. It also has many small branched endings called dendrites, and one wire-like part which is much longer, called an axon. Electrical nerve signals are received from other neurons across tiny gaps, synapses, into the dendrites. The signals travel along the cell's membrane, and into the axon. In turn, this forms synapses with more neurons farther along the system.

BRANCHES EVERYWHERE
The electron microscope shows neurons (green) distinguished from their surrounding cells, showing how their branches form an immense interconnected net. One neuron can have links with more than 1,000 others. Nerve signals can take any path between them, and the possible routes are countless.

Nucleus

Cell membrane

Cell body

Dendrite

Synapse

Nerve cell may be as long as 1 m (40 in)

Axon runs continuously towards nerve ending

Schwann cell wraps around axon

Mitochondrion inside axon (p. 13)

Insulating myelin sheath made by Schwann cell

Oculomotor nerve controls eyeball and iris muscles (pp. 52-53)

Constriction called node of Ranvier

Cerebral cortex of brain (pp. 60-61)

Facial nerves control muscles for facial expressions

FACIAL NERVES
This model shows just a few of the nerves in the face and neck. Most are a combination of sensory and motor, in bundles of cells. The sensory nerves take nerve signals from sight, smell, taste, or touch to the brain. The motor nerves transmit brain signals to instruct the facial muscles to smile or frown, and the neck muscles to move the head. The lingual nerve is solely sensory, carrying touch sensations from the tongue, the floor of the mouth, and the lower jaw. It is as thin as a piece of string, yet it contains as many as 10,000 axons.

Lingual nerve

Salivary gland (pp. 34-35)

FOUNDER OF NEUROLOGY
French physician Jean Martin Charcot (1825-1893) was a leading expert of his time on the nervous system. He recognized several important nerve diseases, such as multiple sclerosis. His interest in hysteria and hypnosis opened the way for the branch of medicine known as psychiatry; among his students was Sigmund Freud (p. 63).

Spinal nerves

The brain

WHEN HUMAN WARRIORS ATE THE BRAINS of their admired enemies to gain their cunning and wisdom, they identified the right organ. Since Plato and Hippocrates of Ancient Greece, the brain has been seen as the seat of intelligence and the soul. One person who disagreed was Aristotle, who believed the soul's home was the heart. His studies on animals correctly showed that the living brain, unlike the skin and other organs, can feel nothing. Aristotle concluded it could not be the site of consciousness. Herophilus of Alexandria, about 300 BC, carried out some of the first recorded studies of the human brain. He identified its main parts, like the cerebrum and cerebellum. He also brought the organ back to prominence as the seat of thought and intelligence. Its major anatomy was established by Renaissance times, and its basic microscopic structure by the 1900s. The marvel of the brain is the way its 100 billion nerve cells interlink via untold trillions of connections.

HOLE IN THE HEAD
Phineas Gage was foreman of a quarrying gang in the USA. In 1848 a gunpowder accident blew a metal rod through his cheek, up through the left frontal lobe of his brain, and out of his skull (above). He lived, the wound healed, but his personality changed from contented and considerate, to obstinate, moody, and foul-mouthed. He was living proof that the front of the brain is involved in aspects of personality.

THE BRAIN SEEN FROM BELOW
The brain's three major parts are the brain stem, the cerebellum, and the cerebrum. In humans the cerebrum is divided into two hemispheres which form nine-tenths of the brain's volume. The brain is only one-fiftieth of the body's weight, and yet it receives about one-fifth of the blood supply (pp. 30-33). Arteries to the brain form a ring called the circle of Willis, which may be a bypass route should one vessel become blocked.

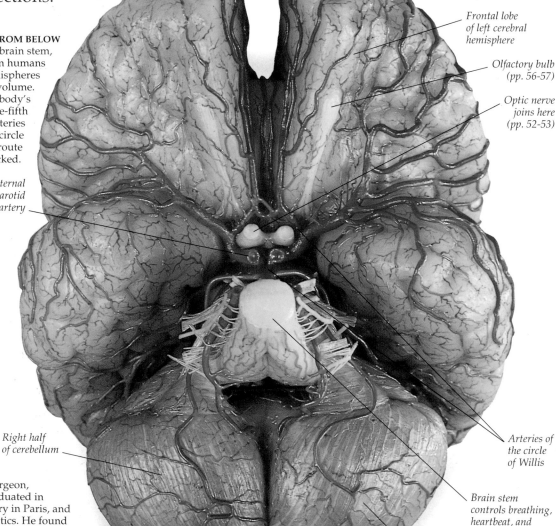

Front of brain

Frontal lobe of left cerebral hemisphere

Olfactory bulb (pp. 56-57)

Optic nerve joins here (pp. 52-53)

Internal carotid artery

Arteries of the circle of Willis

Right half of cerebellum

Brain stem controls breathing, heartbeat, and digestion

Left half of cerebellum

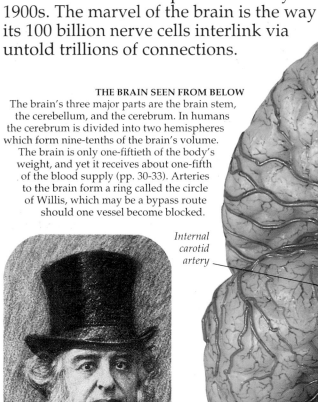

SITE OF SPEECH
Pierre Paul Broca (1824-1880) was a surgeon, anatomist, and anthropologist. He graduated in medicine, became a professor of surgery in Paris, and was also interested in higher mathematics. He found that a small area on the outer layer of the cerebrum is responsible for coordinating the muscles in the voicebox and neck that produce speech. This is now called Broca's area, or the speech motor centre. Broca also studied cancers, and developed instruments for measuring brains and skulls.

LEFT AND RIGHT

In the spinal cord and base of the brain, nerves cross from left to right. This means the left side of the brain receives sensory signals from, and sends motor signals to, the right side of the body, and vice versa. One side of the brain usually dominates, and this relates to a person's "handedness". The left side dominates in right handers, it has Broca's area for example, and in left-handed people, Broca's area is generally found on the right cerebral hemisphere. Left-handed people often excel in the visual, musical, and the creative arts, such as extraordinary rock guitarist Jimi Hendrix (1942-1970), who held his right-handed guitar upside down.

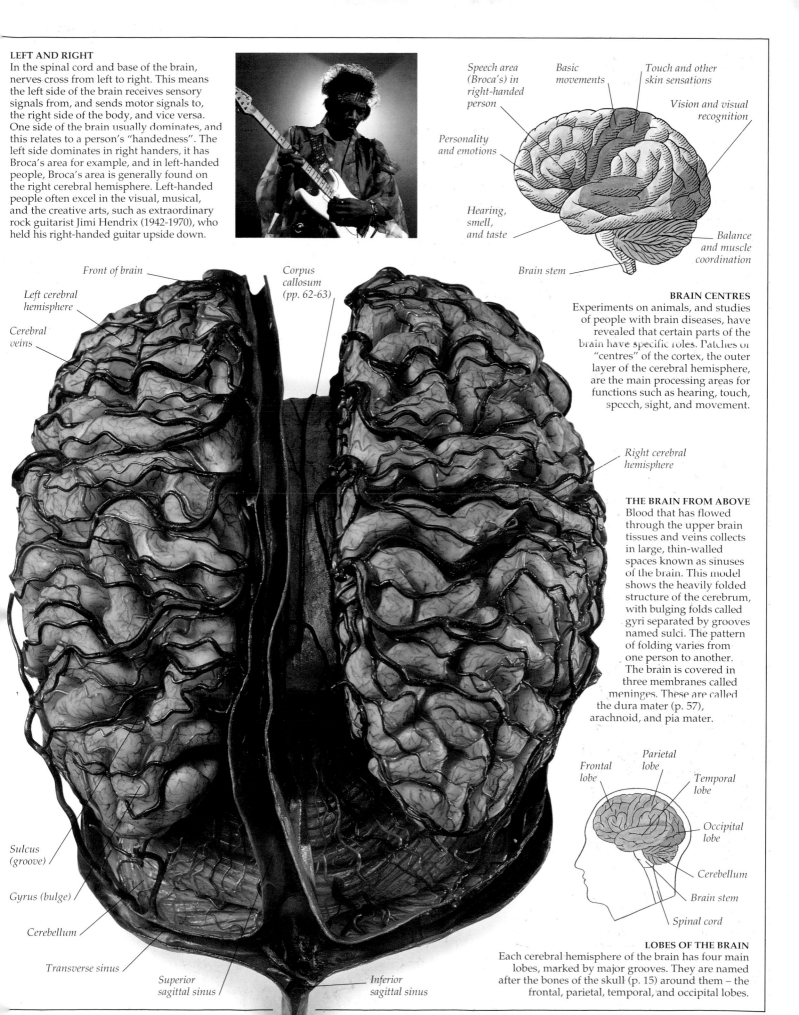

Speech area (Broca's) in right-handed person

Basic movements

Touch and other skin sensations

Vision and visual recognition

Personality and emotions

Hearing, smell, and taste

Balance and muscle coordination

Brain stem

Front of brain

Corpus callosum (pp. 62-63)

Left cerebral hemisphere

Cerebral veins

Right cerebral hemisphere

Sulcus (groove)

Gyrus (bulge)

Cerebellum

Transverse sinus

Superior sagittal sinus

Inferior sagittal sinus

BRAIN CENTRES

Experiments on animals, and studies of people with brain diseases, have revealed that certain parts of the brain have specific roles. Patches of "centres" of the cortex, the outer layer of the cerebral hemisphere, are the main processing areas for functions such as hearing, touch, speech, sight, and movement.

THE BRAIN FROM ABOVE

Blood that has flowed through the upper brain tissues and veins collects in large, thin-walled spaces known as sinuses of the brain. This model shows the heavily folded structure of the cerebrum, with bulging folds called gyri separated by grooves named sulci. The pattern of folding varies from one person to another. The brain is covered in three membranes called meninges. These are called the dura mater (p. 57), arachnoid, and pia mater.

Frontal lobe

Parietal lobe

Temporal lobe

Occipital lobe

Cerebellum

Brain stem

Spinal cord

LOBES OF THE BRAIN

Each cerebral hemisphere of the brain has four main lobes, marked by major grooves. They are named after the bones of the skull (p. 15) around them – the frontal, parietal, temporal, and occipital lobes.

Inside the brain

THIS BOOK BEGAN BY COMPARING THE HUMAN BODY with its fellow mammals, and finding it similar – except for the brain. Recent scientific research seems to be confirming that in this organ reside the secrets of consciousness, thoughts, reasoning, intelligence, memory, language, and other aspects of our unique "human-ness". Influential French philosopher and mathematician René Descartes (1596-1650) proposed a theory of the universe as a giant clockwork-type machine of minute particles of "matter", moving according to mechanical principles. However, he said the human being was a combination of two kinds of substances: body (matter) and mind, a thinking substance. The body existed and could be measured. The mind was different. It thought, sensed, and willed. The link between the two was the pineal gland, deep in the brain. Through the pineal, said Descartes, the mind influenced parts of the brain. The effects travelled through the fluid ventricle chambers and along the nerves, to produce muscle movements. Since Descartes' time, the relationship of body and mind has been an endless source of discussion and fascination for philosophers and scientists alike.

LIQUID INTELLIGENCE?
Galen correctly said that the brain's abilities could be attributed to the various regions of its solid parts. For centuries mainstream opinion had placed more importance on the pale yellow cerebrospinal fluid in the brain's ventricles, or inner chambers. This diagram from the 17th century links each chamber, or "cell", with a mental quality such as imagination, or interpreting the senses.

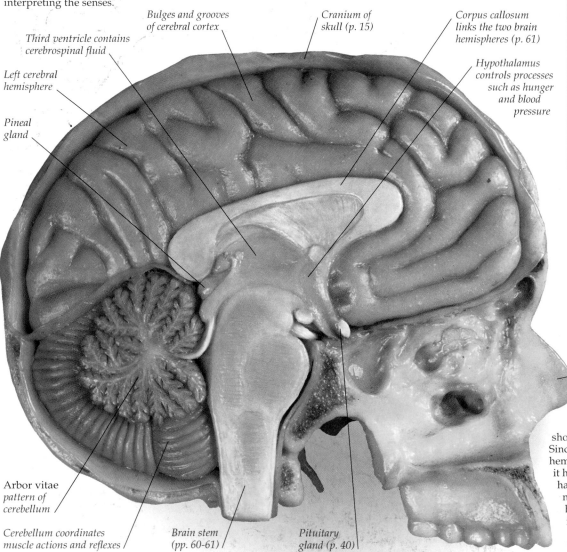

Bulges and grooves of cerebral cortex

Cranium of skull (p. 15)

Corpus callosum links the two brain hemispheres (p. 61)

Third ventricle contains cerebrospinal fluid

Hypothalamus controls processes such as hunger and blood pressure

Left cerebral hemisphere

Pineal gland

Arbor vitae pattern of cerebellum

Cerebellum coordinates muscle actions and reflexes

Brain stem (pp. 60-61)

Pituitary gland (p. 40)

Nose bone of skull (p. 15)

A MAZE OF NERVE SIGNALS
Brain tissue is made up of billions of neurons, each with thousands of synaptic connections (p. 59), and support cells, providing mechanical and metabolic servicing for them. This micrograph shows five star-shaped astrocytes, support cells in the brain's "grey matter". A recent discovery shows that these cells may play a role in changing neuron connections according to outside stimulations, which could be the basis of memory.

LOOKING INSIDE THE BRAIN
In this model the head is cut down the centre, between the eyes, showing the central slice of the brain. Since the inner side of the cerebral hemisphere curves down to the midline, it has not been cut; the corpus callosum has. This bridge of over 100 million nerve fibres links the two sides of the brain (p. 61). The cerebellum shows its folded structure that produces a branching pattern known as the *arbor vitae* or "tree of life".

DEEP SLEEP
French painter Henri Rousseau (1844-1910) introduced unreal, dream-like, and often slightly comic qualities to much of his work, like *The Sleeping Gypsy*. A mixture of recognizable figures in strange situations and odd settings, often from the very recent past, occurs in the dreams of many people. One explanation is that the dreaming brain is fast-replaying recent events. It stores "significant" ones in the memory banks and discards others, even if the significance is not obvious to the dreamer. Dreams seem to happen at a deep, primitive level and have been called the "core of the unconscious".

DEEP THOUGHT
Auguste Rodin (p. 6) portrayed pensive concentration in his statue of *The Thinker*. Recent research shows that conscious awareness of our surroundings is largely based on sight (pp. 52-53). When humans want to concentrate on thought processes, they "stare into space", almost unseeing, so that inner mental processes come to the fore. This phenomenon is almost unique to humans.

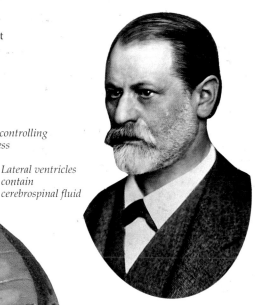

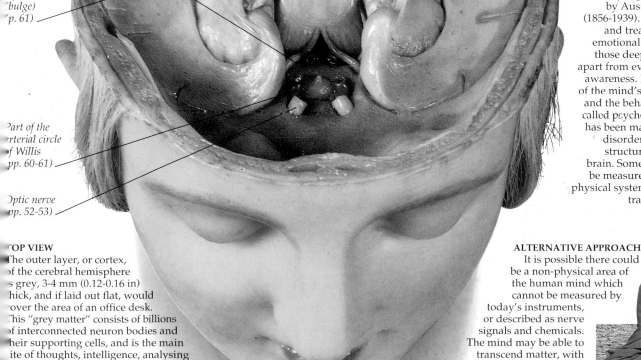

Grey matter of
cerebral cortex

White matter of
cerebral cortex

Oculomotor nerve
controls eyeball
muscles, iris, and
lens (pp. 52-53)

Sulcus
(groove)
(p. 61)

Gyrus
(bulge)
(p. 61)

Part of the
arterial circle
of Willis
(pp. 60-61)

Optic nerve
(pp. 52-53)

Fourth
ventricle

Brain stem

Part of limbic system controlling
emotions and awareness

Lateral ventricles
contain
cerebrospinal fluid

MATTERS OF THE MIND
One field of medicine to emerge recently is psychiatry, pioneered by Austrian Sigmund Freud (1856-1939). It involves the study and treatment of mental and emotional problems, especially those deep in the unconscious, apart from everyday thinking and awareness. Its counterpart study of the mind's "normal" processes, and the behaviour that results, is called psychology. Great progress has been made in linking mental disorders to abnormalities of structure or chemistry in the brain. Some day thoughts might be measured as a Descartes-like physical system of electrical signals travelling along nerves.

TOP VIEW
The outer layer, or cortex, of the cerebral hemisphere is grey, 3-4 mm (0.12-0.16 in) thick, and if laid out flat, would cover the area of an office desk. This "grey matter" consists of billions of interconnected neuron bodies and their supporting cells, and is the main site of thoughts, intelligence, analysing the signals from the senses, and initiating movements. The "white matter" beneath is mainly bundles of nerve fibres, encased in insulating myelin sheaths (pp. 58-59).

ALTERNATIVE APPROACH
It is possible there could be a non-physical area of the human mind which cannot be measured by today's instruments, or described as nerve signals and chemicals. The mind may be able to transcend matter, with techniques such as meditation. With so much anatomical and physiological knowledge, these are questions for future body scientists.

Index

Acknowledgments

Dorling Kindersley would like to thank:

Dr M. C. E. Hutchinson, Department of Anatomy, United Medical and Dental Schools of Guy's and St Thomas's Hospitals for skeletal material on pages 15, 46cr, 49cl, 55tr; Old Operating Theatre Museum, London, for the loan of surgical tools on pages 10-11, 47cl; Dr K. Clark, Department of Haematology, Guy's Hospital, for help in preparing blood samples on page 33t; Steve Gorton and assistant Sarah Ashun for special photography on pages 10-11, 15, 33t, 46cr, 47cl, 49cl, 55tr; Alex Arthur for assistance in Italy. Thanks also to British Museum for mummy (pp. 8-9); Peter Chadwick, Geoff Dann, Philip Dowell, Peter Hayman, and Dave King for additional photography; Bob Gordon for design assistance; Sharon Jacobs for proofreading;

Catherine O'Rourke for additional picture research.

Models on pages 16cr, 17tc, 19tl, 22cl, 26bc, 32r, 38bl, 38br, 42b, 43b, 44, 45bl, 46bl, 48, 51c, 56c supplied by Somso Modelle, Coburg, Germany.

Illustrations Alan Jackson
Retouching Nick Oxtoby/Tapestry
Index Jane Parker

Picture credits
t=top b=bottom c=centre l=left r=right

Allsport 19br; 35tr.
Bettmann Archive 37tl; 48tl; 49cr; 58bl; 63cr.
Ron Boardman 19bl; 22br.
Bridgeman Art Library/Basle 30tl; /Bibliotheque Nationale 8cr; /Bodleian

Library 9cl; 10tl; 49br; /British Library 37br; /British Museum 36tl; /Louvre 46tl; /Mauritshaus 11tl; /M.O.M.A., N.Y. 63tc; /Musée Condé, Chantilly 44tl; /Musée Rodin 63tl; /Private Collection 6tl; /Royal College of Physicians 30cl.
E. T. Archive 58tl.
Mary Evans Picture Library 6cl; 9tl; 9tr; 12tl; 12c; 14tl; 16cl; 25br; 26tr; 28tl; 28br; 34cl; 38tr; 40tl; 43tl; 50l; 51tr; 52; 54tl; 55br; 58cl.
Robert Harding Picture Library 8tl; 10c; 23tl; 38tl.
Hulton Deutsch Collection 11tr; 22tl; 23br; 24br; 28tr; 32cl; 32b; 52tl; 54tr.
Image Bank/M.di Giacomo 21tl.
Kobal Collection 32tr; 49tr.
Mansell Collection 38br; 56tl; 59bl; 60bl.
National Medical Slidebank 54bl.
Redferns 24tl; 61tl.
Ann Ronan Collection, Image Select 12b; 14cl; 26cr; 52tr; 62tl.
Science Photo Library 16tl; 24c; 34br; 39tr; 41cl; 41cr; 53br; /Dr Tony Brain 33tr; /Goran Bredburg 55bl; /Jean-Loup Charmet 34bl; /Chemical Design 33cl;

/CNRI 27tl; 39cr; 45tr; /Elscint, CNRI 13br; /Dr Brian Eyden 50cr; /Astrid & Hans Frieder Michler 41tr; /Eric Grave 51cl; /Manfred Kage 17tr; 37bl; /Hank Morgan 62cr; /Professor P. Motta, Dept of Anatomy, La Sapienza, Roma 16bl; 37tr; 43tr; 52br; /Motta, Porter, Andrews 57tr; /Gopal Murti 48tr; /NIBSC 33cr; /Novosti 13bc; /David Parker 63br; /Alfred Pasieka 50tr; /Petit Format, CSI 44cr; /D. Phillips 59tr /David Schart 50bc; /Secchi, Lecaque, Roussel, UCLAF, CNRI 17bc; 41bl; 57tl; /Sinclair Stammer 13tr; 50br.
Warren Museum, Harvard Medical School 60tr.
The Trustee of the Wellcome Trust 7tl; 8cl; 17tl; 20tr; 44tr; 47tl.
Zefa 14bl.

With the exception of the items listed above, and the objects on pages pp. 8-9b, p.12cl, 12cr, 13tl, 26l, 49tc, 49bl, all the photographs in this book are of models in the collection of the Museo della Specola, Florence, Italy.

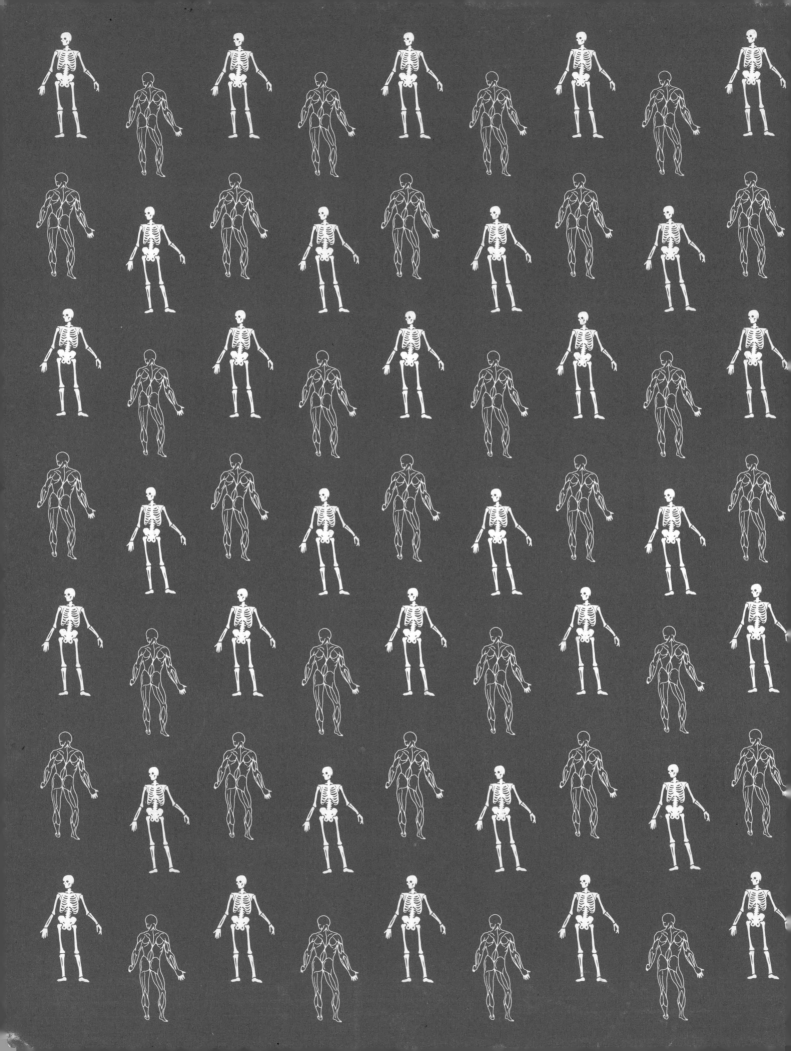